Color

Is

Home

For my mother, Andrea:
my greatest role model and eternal cheerleader.

CHARLOTTE COOTE

Color Is Home

A BRAVE GUIDE TO DESIGNING CLASSIC INTERIORS

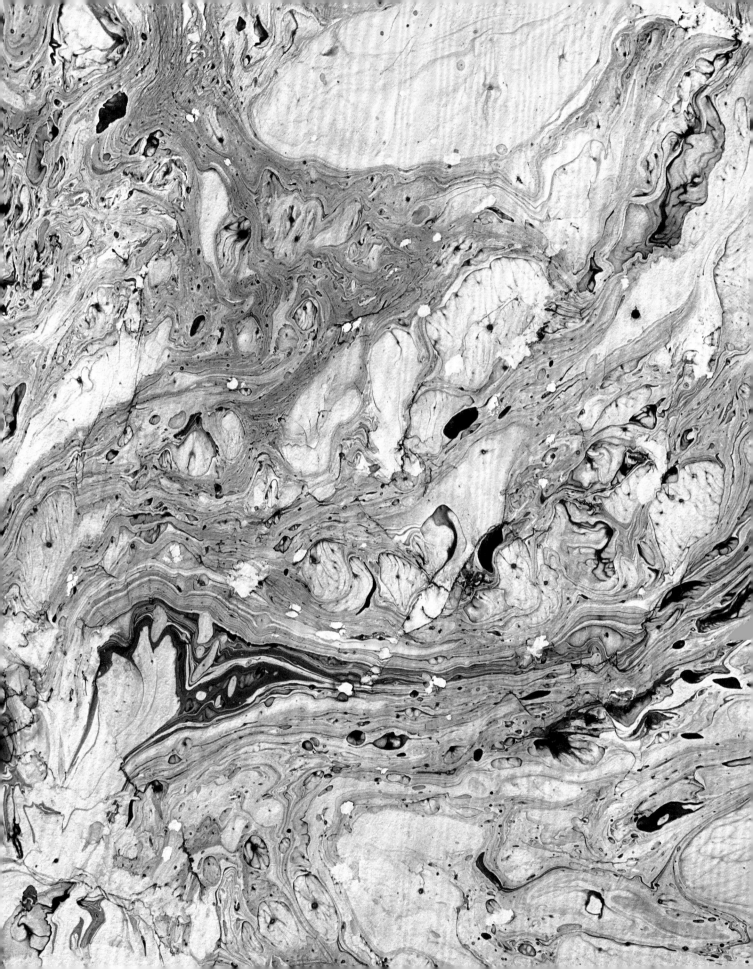

Contents

A NOTE BY NINA CAMPBELL

– 7 –

FOREWORD BY PAUL BANGAY

– 8 –

INTRODUCTION

– 15 –

CHAPTER 01

DESIGN PHILOSOPHY

– 33 –

CHAPTER 02

THE BRIEF

– 57 –

CHAPTER 03

CREATING A NARRATIVE

– 69 –

CHAPTER 04

LIGHT

– 83 –

CHAPTER 05

COLOUR

– 97 –

CHAPTER 06

TEXTILES

– 143 –

CHAPTER 07

FURNITURE LAYOUT

– 169 –

CHAPTER 08

REPURPOSING

– 187 –

CHAPTER 09

OPPOSITES ATTRACT

– 205 –

CHAPTER 10

FAVOURITE BOOKS

– 217 –

ART CREDITS – 222 –

ACKNOWLEDGEMENTS – 223 –

A Note

BY
NINA CAMPBELL

A couple of years ago, I arrived in Melbourne after a long working trip around the United States. Can you imagine anything more joyful and energising than being transported the next morning into the magical domain of Charlotte Coote at her family home, Marnanie?

WINDING UP THE drive and arriving at the house was like being taken back in time. It was a beautiful day; the gardens, shrouded in mist, were at their most romantic. Paul Bangay, a good friend, walked and talked us around the property he had known and worked on for many years.

Charlotte has made a home that is welcoming and comfortable, yet youthful and surprising. After looking at every detail, as only nosy designers do, I sat down to the most delicious lunch in the hot-pink dining room – a room I have been dreaming about ever since!

I am lucky enough to have known Charlotte's father, John Coote, a renowned interior designer of great

taste and knowledge, and am fortunate to have been able to get to know Charlotte and her work. Charlotte has a true passion for design, something that obviously started in childhood but has been honed by reading and digesting all the design greats of the past and adding her inimitable touch. I appreciate her infinite attention to detail, but most of all I love her use of colour and design gleaned from all over the world – and her sense of wit.

As I read her words of wisdom throughout these pages, I find myself nodding in agreement. I wish Charlotte enormous success with this beautiful book.

Foreword

BY
PAUL BANGAY

As a budding garden designer, I spent my days dreaming of magical faraway places: of gardens in milder climates, full of ancient walls and crumbling architecture festooned with old climbing roses, wisteria and other romantic coverings; of regions overseas – England, France and Italy – not scorched by endless summers; and of idyllic locations shrouded much of the year in mist and rain. Such places seemed reachable only via long, expensive plane trips, which l was as yet unable to afford. This all changed the day I met the then custodians of Marnanie – one of Mount Macedon's historic hill station properties – Kevin O'Neill and John Graham.

At the time, I was at college studying landscape design, and a friend of mine worked at Kevin's florist shop in South Yarra, Melbourne. I went to see her there one day and instantly felt at home immersed in the heady glamour of the shop, with its abundance of marble, mirror and flowers, in Kevin's trademark style.

OPPOSITE – *The grand old gates at Marnanie.*

THIS VISIT LED to one of my greatest and longest-lasting friendships, with both Kevin and John. The pair went on to mentor and support me in my early endeavours with gardens and design. They asked me if I would like to do some work in their Mount Macedon garden – I could stay in the house and work in the garden during the day, they offered – and of course I jumped at the opportunity. The magic commenced the moment I approached the front gates via the long, steep gravel drive. Trees overhung the drive, with branches almost touching the ivy-covered ground, to form a tunnel that delivered you from the reality of a bitumen road into another world – a world I had only dreamt of.

In the Marnanie garden, I found the landscape of my dreams: rich mountain soil clothed in spring flowering bulbs, with layers of perennials, exotic shrubs and towering trees such as sequoias. In the manner of ancient European gardens, a spring at the top of the garden was the source of numerous streams that in turn fed the many fountains. It was a garden of cool, moist mountain air, offering a kinder environment for plants than much of the rest of Australia could ever provide. The house was equally as enchanting: dark and moody, yet with theatre lighting dramatically highlighting precious antiques and objets d'art. It was always full of flowers, and for most of the year there was a fire burning in at least one of its many hearths.

OPPOSITE – *The historic house glimpsed through lush ferns.*

ABOVE – *This summer house was designed by Paul Bangay for Kevin O'Neill and John Graham in the 1990s.*

Back then, and indeed to this day, Marnanie was a place for entertaining. Visitors were attracted by the gentle mountain climate of the area, so close to Melbourne, as well as the grand house and famous garden – and Kevin and John were consummate hosts and entertainers. Parties, held outside in summer and indoors by fireside in winter, were plentiful and full of diverse and interesting people. It was a place brimming with love, fun and, above all, great design. Sadly, Kevin died in January 1997 and subsequently the property passed through numerous owners. With each new owner, part of its magic faded away, until finally the house was devoid of regular residents and the garden was maintained just enough to keep it alive.

Walking through the Marnanie garden with John Graham in 2017, when the estate was once again up for sale, we struck upon an idea for who would make the perfect new owner: Charlotte Coote. Charlotte was the daughter of one of my greatest friends and design buddies, John Coote, who had sadly passed away a short while before, and she was looking for a new home. Charlotte had spent some of her childhood in the neighbouring property, Penrith, which her parents then owned, and had attended some of Kevin and John's famous garden parties. A single phone call sealed the deal. We had at last found a worthy custodian for the property.

One of the great joys of my recent life has been to be able to regularly revisit Marnanie and to see new life being breathed into it. I have, again, had the privilege to help with the development of the garden, and it has been wonderful to witness the great enthusiasm Charlotte and her husband, Geordie, have for its restoration and further development. Herbaceous borders are being replanted, the fragrant rhododendron walks are being pruned hard and brought back to life, and, as in Kevin's day, flowers are being grown to harvest for sale at the Melbourne markets.

Spending time at Marnanie over the past few years has also afforded me the opportunity to observe Charlotte's enormous flair for interior design. In renovating the gracious old weatherboard home,

Charlotte has found a way to honour the house's long history, while transforming it into a fresh, light-filled, contemporary space, ideal for a young family. The Edwardian manor is now filled with a mixture of Irish furniture, modern paintings and exciting fabrics. Where once dark wood panelling dominated, white walls now usher in light and create a sense of space. Charlotte is not afraid of colour or pattern and mixes them in ways I have not seen since the 1970s, in the work of famed English interior designer David Hicks. Marnanie, it appears, has been the perfect place for this young designer to experiment, flourish – and reveal her talent to the world. 'Life, fun and happiness' seems to be her mantra, and this is expressed in every room she touches.

ABOVE – *A charming bird tap from the shop Paul had in Melbourne.*

OPPOSITE – *The guest bedroom, painted in Resene Zinzan, with slipper chairs upholstered in Georgia Macmillan Indigo Spot.*

Introduction

*I can clearly remember the feeling I had as I entered
Marnanie's gates, glimpsing that magical white house floating
above the ancient trees, seemingly drawing me towards it.
I knew at that very moment that I wanted this house
to become my family home.*

DESIGNING AND RENOVATING Marnanie has been a project of love that represents the culmination of my life's work to date. Since moving into the historic property in Mount Macedon, Victoria, five years ago, I have come to realise how much my design aesthetic has evolved over time. My personal and professional journey has taken me from one end of the world to the other, and back again. Along the way I've learnt countless design lessons and gained invaluable experience. I wanted to write this book to document those insights – to share the processes and principles I use as the foundation for designing classic contemporary interiors.

Creating a sense of timelessness was my core goal when restoring Marnanie, and it is the philosophy that underpins all my projects. My hope is that this book honours the beauty of timeless design and shares with you my aesthetic and style in an accessible and tangible way.

The day my husband, Geordie, and I first visited Marnanie, we fell hopelessly in love with the place. Built in the 1890s for Sir Isaac Isaacs, the first Australian-born governor-general, the house was tired, but so beautiful. It seemed almost to beckon to me, saying: 'Live here, and I will make you all very happy.' My conviction that this was *the one* really took hold when we reached the towering rhododendron garden at the top of the property, which was surrounded by ancient trees and birdsong. I felt immediately at home.

OPPOSITE – *Me on the croquet lawn in the towering rhododendron garden.*
FOLLOWING – *My home, Marnanie.*

My sense of connection to the place should have come as no surprise, I suppose. I was born at Penrith, a historic hill station property in Mount Macedon, and spent the early years of my life there. Four decades on, with many countries and life experiences in between, my family home is Marnanie, the property right next door. Mine is a story of coming full circle, featuring two historically important houses, both so special to my heart, which stand side by side but have a world between them.

I have had a profound relationship with interior design my whole life. My father was a talented and successful interior designer, so I was born into it, lived alongside it as a child and was taught it growing up. It was inevitable, perhaps, that as an adult I would choose design as my career. I have always felt that good design can fuel your energy and enhance your life. I love the idea of making a place better; of adapting the space to enrich the lives of the people who will use it.

Growing up, family life was never dull. My parents, John and Andrea Coote, loved to entertain, so my siblings and I were constantly surrounded by creative, international and successful people. Our parents instilled in us, from a young age, the notion that style is timeless, and that it is something that should spill into every area of life. Anything deemed 'on trend' was discouraged. This concept became intrinsic to everything I went on to create in my later life. Our parents taught us about beautiful interiors, collecting antiques and art. We were encouraged to read widely – designer biographies were to be found in every room – and to listen to classical music. We travelled extensively throughout Europe and America. It sounds clichéd to say I learnt 'style' growing up, but as children we lived and breathed it, until it became second nature to us. My childhood taught me about style, but also that hard work is the main ingredient for success in life. We were taught not to take our privilege for granted.

Life wasn't always smooth sailing: there were many ups and downs, fuelled largely by my father's eccentric and adventurous spirit. Apart from a few exceptions, we never lived in a house for longer than two years.

Our parents would buy some run-down place, do it up, then sell it. The smell of a freshly painted interior still reminds me of the anticipation I felt when it was time to move on from a completed project to the next adventure. Similarly, the smell of damp books being unpacked evokes the excitement of settling into a new home to begin yet another challenging project.

As a young child in the early 1980s, I lived with my family in Melbourne. It was a time of opulent interior decorating, lavish entertaining, design excess and architectural shoulder pads. My parents were in their element. My mother was an aspiring politician who went on to become a member of the Victorian parliament and built a successful career that spanned two decades. Mum has always had an incredible positivity and the ability to light up a room. People adore and gravitate towards her because she makes them feel as if they are the most important person who ever existed.

My mother has always been glamorous. In terms of fashion, she has really owned every decade, looking equally as chic in her 1980s power suits as she does today in the latest Saint Laurent ensemble from Le Louvre. The same can be said of her homes, which are invariably beautifully styled and curated with a sense of timelessness. She uses only the best textiles and selects beautiful art, complementing these with interesting objects collected on her many travels. She buys the best Irish linen sheets and her vases are always generously filled. The silverware gleams. Interesting books line the shelves, all of which she will have read. Her interiors are never overdone – clutter doesn't belong in her world, on any level.

OPPOSITE – *My family, dressed in true 1983 fashion for my aunt's wedding in Melbourne. I'm the smaller of the two flower girls.*

My first memory of 'design' per se comes from the time our family was living at South Yarra's grand Poolman House in Melbourne. It was 1986, I was six, and my father was in the process of restoring and decorating the entire house. One night I went to visit him in his study as he worked. I vividly remember Dad showing me the textile he had chosen for decorating my bedroom – he explained that he would be using it to upholster the walls and bedhead, and also for the curtains and bedspread. I recall having a very strong feeling of anger and distaste. I didn't like the fabric he had chosen and I told him so. Incredibly, he passed the textile books to me and said, 'Well, here you go then, pet. You find something more suitable.' I quickly went about choosing a delightful high-quality pink chintz with an off-white background. I remember feeling so proud once the room was completed. Even as a six-year-old, I was enchanted by the notion that my choices could make a room more beautiful and joyful to live in. I still have the original bedspread – a reminder of my very first foray into design.

ABOVE – *My childhood bedroom at Poolman House, covered in the pink chintz I selected.*

OPPOSITE – *My bedspread from Poolman House.*

ABOVE – *Bellamont Forest, seen through the giant old beech and oak trees.*

OPPOSITE – *Our Irish wolf hounds, Dolly (front) and Possum (behind). These were also some of the nicknames my father used for me and my siblings.*

– 22 –

During my father's later career as an interior designer, he worked on high-end projects around the globe. As a young boy growing up in Victoria's Wimmera region, Dad had a grand vision for his future, and he had the courage to go after it. His first really big achievement was purchasing the Coote ancestral house in Ireland, in 1985. However, our family's journey to Ireland didn't begin until several years later, when I was eight. That year, the family relocated from Melbourne to Los Angeles. True to my father's erratic nature, one minute we were living at the Beverly Hills Hotel, scouting for schools and a family home, and the next minute the budget had run out and we were forced to move to a far less salubrious hotel in Hollywood. Evidently, Dad's plans in LA fell through, because before we had time to catch our breaths, we were on a plane to Ireland to set up a life in an 18th-century Georgian mansion.

The estate was called Bellamont Forest. The house was designed by architect Sir Edward Lovett Pearce and built, in 1729, for his cousin Sir Thomas Coote, an ancestor of our family. The house is architecturally significant as it was the first example of a Palladian-style villa in Ireland. The original structure and form of the building has never been modified, so it retains the perfect symmetry of the architect's design. It is rumoured that Lovett Pearce met and was influenced by Italian Renaissance architect Andrea Palladio, and that Bellamont Forest was inspired by Palladio's Villa Rotonda in Veneto, Italy. It was my father's dream to restore the house to its full glory.

I lived with my family at the estate for the next four years. Being immersed in the extraordinary and significant architecture of Bellamont had a lasting impact on me. Living in the house, and observing my father sensitively renovate it, I learnt the foundations of good architecture and design. I gained an appreciation of perfect symmetry, proportion and scale. I developed an understanding of how a house can be designed to maximise natural light, in both the summer and winter months.

Surrounded by 1000 acres (400 hectares) of woodlands and lakes, growing up at Bellamont was a child's delight. My sister, Amelia, and I went to the charming national school, along with sixty local children, where we learnt Gaelic. On weekends, I took my horse, Jubilee, on hunts with the county Fermanagh Harriers – which was both a terrifying

and exhilarating experience. At home, we always had Labradors and Irish wolfhounds swirling around, as my father liked the way they colour-coordinated with the house. The place was a magnet for the many interesting and unconventional friends my parents had accumulated over the years, and we were rarely without visitors.

ABOVE – *The ballroom at Bellamont Forest. The artwork is a reproduction
of* The Death of Dido *by Guercino.*

OPPOSITE – *Me with my siblings, Amelia and Angus, in the drawing room at Bellamont
Forest, attending our father's sixtieth birthday party in June 2009.*

– 24 –

The extraordinary English designer David Hicks became a truly important mentor to Dad over many years. David shared with my father his incredible depth of knowledge around 18th- and 19th-century design. In addition, he introduced Dad to the Irish aristocracy, who welcomed my father into the homes their families had occupied for hundreds of years. Dad gained immeasurable knowledge from these experiences. In turn, his superb restoration of Lovett Pearce's Palladian villa became the springboard to his international career. His renown as 'Mr Coote of Cootehill' used to make us laugh, but clients lapped it up. Dad had certainly come a long way since the days of his boyhood in the Wimmera.

ABOVE – *Bellamont Forest's portico entrance is framed by Doric columns made from limestone, with an entablature featuring metopes with carved musical instruments. The building's facade showcases the symmetry and perfect proportions of the original design.*

RIGHT – *Charlotte and Amelia's bedroom at Bellamont Forest.*

OPPOSITE – *The drawing room, designed by my father. The walls are a custom Porter's Paints pink, applied by brush to achieve an aged finish. The hand-carved console, also designed by my father, includes elements based on various architectural adornments of the house itself.*

At the age of twelve, I returned to Australia with my mother and sister, joining my brother, Angus, who was at boarding school. Meanwhile, my father stayed on in Ireland to build his design business. For the next six years, I attended a regional boarding school, which I loved. One of my first school-holiday jobs was working for famous Melbourne establishment Graham Geddes Antiques. I am still close with Graham and his children, and often buy from them for my design projects. However, as a thirteen-year-old, I found Graham's larger-than-life personality rather intimidating. My job there was to polish the antique furniture with beeswax – not very glamorous, but I worked hard and ended up learning a lot about antiques and antiquities.

After graduating from school, I completed a double degree in business and marketing. Finally, I returned to Bellamont, where I began running the operations of my father's burgeoning interior design business. He was a brilliant designer, and by that time he was beginning to enjoy a lot of international success.

In Europe, Dad and I built houses from the ground up, designed boutique hotels, decorated London apartments, and fashioned and restored privately owned 18th-century houses and castles. For all these projects, we created exquisite products and furnishings from scratch. Dad was a creative genius with a photographic memory, and an aesthetic perfectionist. Working for him during this time, I found the projects satisfyingly diverse, educative and enormous fun. They laid the foundations for my career.

No teacher was as tough, nor as challenging to work for, as my father. But he taught me more about design than anyone else. He taught me about colour and textiles, scale and proportion. He taught me the importance of timelessness and how to create authentic design. He gave me the confidence to create something no one else could. He gave me skills and knowledge I could not have learnt anywhere else. He taught me how to think big.

My father strongly discouraged me from undertaking any formal study of interior design, stating, 'Pet, don't bother. I've taught you everything you need to know!' My father made life less ordinary. He had a wonderful sense of humour and a wild eccentricity. Working together during my twenties, we travelled a lot and we had a lot of good times.

OPPOSITE – *The dining room at Bellamont Forest.*
ABOVE – *My father, John Coote, larger than life, on the day of his sixtieth birthday.*

In 2008, I moved back to Australia and started my own interior design business, Coote & Co. I had the full support of my parents, and of my devoted stepfather, Alan Naylor. Alan is a well-respected investor and stockbroker, with an incredible business mind, and he mentored me in financial literacy.

I started the business with big plans, good skills and plenty of grit, yet I had no idea how difficult it would be to make it a success. I had worked hard to save the money to start my business, but was soon staring down the barrel of the global financial crisis.

I quickly learnt that I could not assume that what had worked for Dad and me in Europe would work in the Australian market – especially in the economic climate at the time. So, I looked for a niche in the market, and adapted my strategy and business goals to attract a high-end clientele. I established an interior design shop in Melbourne, selling premium furniture, antiques, textiles and lighting. I ran the shop for seven years and the most important thing I learnt was to listen to the demands of the market. This understanding led me to take my business to the next stage: I closed the shop and created an interior design studio. The Melbourne studio would focus on classic contemporary interior design for high-end private residential clients.

Establishing the business was challenging, but I had passion and conviction, and I was determined to make it work. I constantly adapted the business formula until I got it on track, then built on my successes to get the studio to where it is today. The successes were of course interspersed with many failures, but I truly believed that if I just kept going, with focus and commitment, and kept trying different ways of making it work, I would succeed. I stuck it out, and it paid off. The journey definitely wasn't easy – especially considering that along the way I had three children in three years, and juggled moving homes and schools.

I would describe my design style as 'new classicist': based on traditional foundations but with a strong twist of contemporary and the unexpected. I aim to work with art, architecture and objects of quality to create timeless designs – either classic or contemporary. I am on a constant quest to uncover the unusual, the unique and the rare. I don't believe in fads or anything remotely trendy. I revere timelessness above all else: the luxury of a house that never dates and only gets better with age. I have found this to be the one ingredient all my clients crave. Every time I create, I am guided by the core principles of my design philosophy. In addition to being timeless, interiors and their contents must be authentic, good quality, generous and comfortable. I know that if I am true to these principles, good design will follow.

Geordie and I, and our three daughters, have now lived at Marnanie for five years. Restoring the garden and house has certainly been taxing – on our time, resources and creativity. When we moved there in 2017, the property was very run down and we knew it was an enormous project – and a huge responsibility – to take on. However, we felt ready for the challenge. We saw the potential to create a wonderful family home, in a beautiful country setting, where our girls could learn and grow. We continue to remind ourselves of how each small goal we achieve benefits us as a family. And as the house and garden slowly awaken from their long slumber, they give us happiness in spades. We are proud to be custodians of something so special and hope many more generations will continue to enjoy the beauty of this unique place.

Today, as I regard my childhood home Penrith, and my family home, Marnanie, still standing side by side, I see between them four decades of learning and life experience. This book is the result of the hard work, successes and mistakes of those decades, and represents everything I have learnt to become the person and designer I am now. I hope that you can draw inspiration from this book and that it helps you create design that is timeless, unique and authentic to you.

OPPOSITE – *My husband, Geordie, and me with our daughters, Sybil, Daphne and Francesca, and our Labrador, Bobby.*

Design Philosophy

CHAPTER 01

Design Philosophy

Before commencing a project or making a new purchase,
I like to revisit the core principles of my design philosophy.
It helps me to focus on, create and invest in the product and design,
in order to achieve enduring style. It is like rereading a mission
statement to remind myself what it is, aesthetically, I'm setting out to
achieve. Whether choosing a single cushion or redecorating an entire
home, the five principles I always consider are:

—

TIMELESSNESS
AUTHENTICITY
LIFESTYLE
SCALE
&
QUALITY

PREVIOUS — *The custom banquet seat I designed for the Coote & Co. office, upholstered in Bird and Thistle by Brunschwig & Fils.*

OPPOSITE — *For my wedding, I adapted an Irish Georgian console into a dining table that could seat the entire bridal party. Many years later, the piece was painted in high-gloss Resene Cupid pink. It is now my office desk.*

Timelessness

DESIGN PRINCIPLE
NO. 01

*Timeless design is not only stylish now but will remain so in twenty
or more years. Such designs are usually original, bespoke and good quality.
They reflect a personality or narrative that holds special meaning.*

*There are several important factors to consider when setting
out to create timeless design.*

TRENDS

AVOID TRENDS. TRENDS tend to develop from one great design that is adapted and developed by others, and then rolled out en masse. Remember the Scandinavian interior design movement of the early 2000s? Although the style had its foundations in established high-end design, its authenticity was diminished once department stores got involved. Many products made and sold during that period were cheap reproductions of iconic designs by famous furniture makers. Inevitably, the mass market tired of the look once it appeared in every second home. The Scandi craze provides a perfect example of why it is not a good idea to do what everyone else is doing when it comes to design.

ICONIC PIECES

LOOK FOR ICONIC pieces. An iconic piece is a must-have or go-to piece that exudes infinite style: a great-quality brass standard lamp, for example, or a Murano glass ceiling light. It is classic, beautiful, well made and will never date. It's important to note that 'iconic' doesn't necessarily equate with 'antique'. Just because something is old, doesn't necessarily mean it is timeless. Conversely, something new can have a timeless quality about it – like great contemporary art. The trick, of course, is learning how to sort the good from the bad. Iconic pieces make great investments, as they can be reimagined in a multitude of settings.

COST

TIMELESSNESS DOESN'T HAVE to cost a fortune. Items purchased at auction or from second-hand shops can represent incredible value for money, especially when they are well made and not likely to be found elsewhere. With a little care and some new fabric, a tired old armchair can be transformed into something spectacular and unique. It's about mixing high with low, as well as old with new, to create charm and a sense of narrative.

For example, I once purchased a lovely cane sofa for $10 at a little-known auction house and reupholstered it in an elegant Colefax and Fowler print.

OPPOSITE – A late 18th-century French ormolu-mounted kingwood, walnut and tulipwood bombe commode, in the Louis XV style, with serpentine marble top, from Graham Geddes Antiques – complemented by contemporary artwork by Celia Perceval.

Be faithful to your own taste, because nothing you really like is ever out of style.

– Billy Baldwin

EDUCATING THE EYE

To learn how to make good design choices, you must first educate your eye — that is, you must research and learn as much about classic design as you can.

BOOKS

Read and collect books on early timeless designers you admire (I particularly like David Hicks, Syrie Maugham and Billy Baldwin). Go back to these at the commencement of a project for inspiration or direction. If a book you like references other designers or creatives, make a point of learning more about them.

SHOPS AND AUCTION HOUSES

Visit reputable antique stores, classic interior design shops, textile houses and auction houses. Even if you cannot afford some of the pieces, you will gain inspiration and education.

ONLINE AUCTION HOUSES

When you are unable to attend auctions in person, spend time browsing online auction catalogues. By osmosis, you will learn about furniture and decorative art history. It is also an excellent way to find inspiration and flag potential purchases.

MARKETS

Whether local or international, markets can be treasure chests brimming with unique pieces. Famous markets like Les Puces at Porte de Clignancourt in Paris are amazing to visit, even if you are not looking to buy.

TRAVEL

When you travel, research and visit local artisans (textile makers, artists and furniture makers). Not only will you learn about their manufacturing processes, but you may gain inspiration for future projects.

ARCHITECTURE

Read about (or even better, visit) examples of classic architecture like Andrea Palladio's villas of the Veneto in Italy or the 16th-century Amber Fort in Rajasthan, India. Photograph elements of buildings (famous or not) that you find interesting, for later reference.

INHERITED PIECES

It's worth taking a close look at any family heirlooms. Even ugly or unusual pieces, when thoughtfully restored or repurposed, can add sentiment, charm and personality to your interior.

ABOVE — *An antique marble horse head sits alongside a bone box from India, a speckled Bragg & Co. lamp, a silver vase from Bellamont Forest and a contemporary artwork by Alexandra Brownlow. Mixing items of various styles and origin creates an interesting space.*

OPPOSITE — *Photos from my travels through India, an endless source of inspiration.*

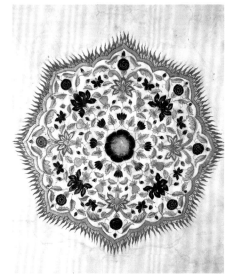

Authenticity

DESIGN PRINCIPLE
NO. 02

Authenticity is all about inventing your own style. It is about incorporating an element of surprise or something unique into a space. Bringing personality and character into an aesthetic is what will set your interior apart from the next.

ONE WAY TO achieve authenticity is to use items that hold meaning for you. You don't want it to appear as if your pieces have all rolled off the back of one truck, or been purchased from a single shop. By gathering antiques, original art, photographs and furniture over time, you can gradually form an interesting collection from which to create your interiors.

RIGHT — An antique oak dresser filled with collected curiosities is a reflection of our clients' style and character.

OPPOSITE — A selection of our clients' military hats, displayed in their private study (top left); curiosities collected by our clients on their travels to Sri Lanka and other international destinations (top right, bottom left); shelves filled with precious books and objects gathered over a lifetime (bottom right).

The best rooms have something to say about the people who live in them.

– *David Hicks*

Lifestyle

DESIGN PRINCIPLE
NO. 03

*Before purchasing or creating anything new, consider the
required functionality of the space you will be working with.
It is important to understand that two different owners of the same
property will likely use it in entirely different ways. In order to create
an interior for maximum usability and enjoyment, you must first
consider who is going to be using the space, and how.*

WHEN WE PURCHASED Marnanie, my aim was to create a home for me and my husband to live in and enjoy with our three young children and a lively puppy. The home's dark, moody aesthetic had suited the previous owners, who only visited on occasional weekends. However, it would not suit the full-time living requirements of a young family. I set out to create a bright and light, durable family home, which would be as lovely in the summer months as in the depths of a snowy mountain winter. I first considered the specific needs of our family and then designed a home that could cope with everything we'd throw at it: from muddy boots and dogs to active young children and their multitudinous toys, from parties and entertaining friends to everyday tasks. I also kept in mind how I might easily adapt things as my children grew up and our needs changed.

BEFORE CREATING ANY SPACE, CONSIDER THE FOLLOWING FACTORS:

PRACTICALITY – Who will use the space?

LIFESTYLE – How and when will the space be used?

EMOTION – How should the space make you feel?

OPPOSITE – *My daughters, Daphne, Sybil and Francesca, at Marnanie.*

FOLLOWING – *The flower room at Marnanie – perfect for storing muddy boots and warm coats.*

Scale

DESIGN PRINCIPLE
NO. 04

I like the word 'generous' when used to describe the scale of an interior space. It suggests a sense of comfort and abundance, which is something I always set out to achieve. However, it is important to consider not only the scale of the space itself but also the scale of various aspects of the interior – including windows, art, lighting and furnishings. The proportion of all elements must be in balance with the size of the room. When working with a sizeable room, for example, it is important to use large or oversized pieces of furniture to complement the scale of the space.

WHEN IT COMES to selecting key pieces of furniture, I almost always choose the option that is a little larger rather than a little smaller. A large piece of furniture can be balanced with a smaller accent piece, like a slipper chair or side table. As a rule, it is better to use a few large pieces of furniture rather than many smaller pieces. Even in a small room, larger pieces of furniture will make the space feel generous.

My father would often refer to a sofa or armchair as being 'too mean'– in other words, too small or uncomfortable – which would make me laugh. He was a large man and therefore favoured a good-quality, oversized armchair. On his visits to my retail shop in Melbourne, I would regularly find him sitting in the generous armchair in the window display. He would read there for hours and quite often fall asleep, which passers-by found highly entertaining. I have since named that armchair model The John Coote chair, as it is generous and comfortable, just as he liked.

OPPOSITE – *Coote & Co.'s Melbourne apartment: John Coote armchair, upholstered in Coote & Co. Bellamont Forest; Roman blinds in Brunschwig & Fils Upton Damask Linen; walls in Hog Bristle Half by Dulux.*

ABOVE – *The Coote & Co. Deco day bed, at one of our Portsea projects, upholstered in Coote & Co. Lough Eske Ivory; cushion in Schumacher Teton. The artwork is part of the* Tree Studies *series (2004) by Robert Doble.*

Quality

DESIGN PRINCIPLE
NO. 05

Investing in quality pieces made by skilled craftspeople will ensure your interiors stand the test of time. Whether a handmade sofa, commissioned artwork or beautiful antique, quality pieces will deliver longevity and timelessness. Always try to buy the best quality you can afford within your budget.

ALTERNATIVELY, CONSIDER RESTORING a tired or damaged piece of high-quality furniture – perhaps something you already own or that you've found in a second-hand shop. If the bones are good, simply applying a coat of paint or reupholstering with a fresh textile can give an old piece a new lease of life.

RIGHT – *A beautiful oak and leather monogrammed desk I designed with Melbourne cabinet-maker Robert Brown.*

OPPOSITE – *The entrance hall at Marnanie, featuring the Coote & Co. Blackwater console, an antique Chinese chair, and prints of works by 18th-century Irish artist Robert Healy (from his Conolly family series).*

OPPOSITE & ABOVE –

An antique Welsh oak dresser (c. 1800), holding my collection of Astier de Villatte ceramics.
The back of the dresser is painted in Hailstorm by Porter's Paints.

– 55 –

THE
Brief

CHAPTER 02

The Brief

It is common for clients I work with to feel a little overwhelmed at the start of a new project, and to be unsure where to begin. Often they know, at heart, what they want, but lack the confidence – or are unable – to articulate the overall look and feel they wish to achieve. To assist clients to clarify their ideas, I designed a set of questions to generate what I call The Brief. The answers to these questions help me to structure a plan and create a narrative for the project. They create a foundation upon which the creative process can take hold and develop.

COOTE & CO.
BRIEFING QUESTIONNAIRE

1. What is the goal of this project?

2. What is the architectural style of your home?

3. What are the most important design changes you want to make in your home – for example: colour, space, comfort, light, storage, artwork, durability?

4. What aesthetic do you hope to achieve? Please provide some visual inspiration or a Pinterest board, including examples of interiors and architecture, and pictures of travel, fashion, art and lifestyle.

5. Summer, autumn, winter or spring?

6. How do you see yourself finding joy and spending time in the completed space? What inspired you to want to live like this?

7. What colours, patterns and materials would you like to see used in this project?

8. What colours, patterns and materials *don't* you like?

9. Do you have existing furniture, rugs or lighting you wish to use in the space?

10. How would you like to feel at the completion of this project?

OPPOSITE – *1. Schumacher Mohave Indigo; 2. International Floor Coverings Coron Cream Abaca; 3. Raoul Textiles Java Indigo; 4. Janus et Cie Ravella Vellum; 5. Bespoke Coote & Co. Blue/White Diamond Rug.*

BREAKWATER

JODPHUR BLUE

BODU

Creating the Brief

When my husband, Geordie, and I purchased Marnanie, we were excited by the idea of transforming this historic property into a family home for ourselves and our three children. The house itself had excellent bones, with generous windows and French doors that opened onto beautiful vistas, and fireplaces in abundance. There was plenty of potential. However, the house was dark and somewhat rundown.

THERE WERE SO many factors to consider before I could think about getting started on the renovation. Some things I knew instinctively, straight away. I knew that my main focus needed to be on bringing a sense of lightness to the home. I would add energy and warmth using colour and layers of texture. I needed to consider the era and history of the property, while bringing the house into the current day. The home also needed to be practical for my young family, with comfort and liveability the priority.

I knew that the process would take place over several years, so I would need to prioritise. First order of business would be to address the walls, flooring, furniture and window treatments. More extensive kitchen and bathroom renovations would follow later. The overgrown garden would also need to be attended to – culled initially, then gradually brought back to life over the coming years.

As is the case for so many of my clients, the difficulty was knowing where to start. I decided to follow my own advice and complete the Coote & Co. Briefing Questionnaire. This process allowed me to more clearly understand and articulate the kind of home

I wished to create. Answering the questions really helped me to narrow my focus and identify not only what inspired me visually but also how we, as a family, wanted to live at Marnanie and what we wanted from the property. With this knowledge, I was able to form a solid plan and a clear scope of works.

Each of the briefing questions provides insight into a client's emotional and practical reasons for undertaking a project. By better understanding the client's perspective, I am able to achieve a design specifically tailored to their wants and needs.

Asking the client to create a folio of inspirational imagery is a key part of the briefing process, as it helps them to express their desired aesthetic. I interpret and add to this folio to form a visual brief for the project.

Following are mood boards for two recent Coote & Co. projects: the first is for Marnanie; the second is for a home in Noosa, Queensland.

MISS CHARLOTTE M.

AND

MR. GEORGE IA

TUTU

PRETTY IN PINK

BIRTHDAY CANDLE

ROSEWOOD

Chinese Chairs.

DGE

NT MACEDON 3441

Dear Charlotte and Georgie,

Very much looking

CAPER

LICHEN

IMPROMPTU ENGLISH PICNIC

SNOW PEA

APPLE CRUNCH

CAPRIOSKA

WASABI

Creating

A

Narrative

CHAPTER 03

Creating a Narrative

Creating the 'narrative' for your project is where the fun starts.
Before you even begin to contemplate colour, textiles or furniture, it is
essential to decide on an overall theme or story. The narrative is what
forms the heart of the design. If a narrative is strong, it can really
elevate the look and feel of a completed space.

OPPOSITE – *1. Rose Tarlow Matchsticks Lagoon; 2. Fabrics from Nicholas Herbert Linoteca range;*
3. Soane Tendril Vine Emerald; 4. Soane Tendril Vine Walnut and Sage; 5. Soane Celestial Square Chestnut; 6. Chelsea Textiles
Mafalda Alga Marina; 7. Chelsea Textiles Cupid in Leaf; 8. Inchyra Beaumont Check Wool Sage; 9. Colefax and Fowler Appledore
Check Beige; 10. Rose Tarlow Paloma Coralline/Natural; 11. Fermoie Nut Brown Wicker; 12. Rose Tarlow Gigi Terre.

Identifying a Theme

There are many ways to identify a project narrative or theme.
For starters, try standing in the house, or on its future site, and
looking at the surrounding landscape. What do you see? What is
the local climate like throughout the seasons? What is the history
of the area? Often the answers to such questions can help form
a narrative for your project to follow.

WHEN IT CAME time to design the new kitchen at Marnanie, the first thing I did was just stand in the space for some time and look around. I wanted to understand the light in the room and also consider what could be seen through the windows. The view through the glass was green, green and more green. Specifically, I could see rhododendrons, a chestnut tree, *Dicksonia* tree ferns, a monkey puzzle tree and mollis azaleas. I knew from experience that the colour of the landscape wouldn't change much over the seasons. I went outside and picked handfuls of leaves, arranged them on the floor in the space and selected a green colour that related to them all: Mount Macedon Green, I called it. I decided to paint all the kitchen joinery in this colour. This reminded me of the quintessential English Georgian country kitchen, in which joinery was often painted. And from here my narrative was born.

OPPOSITE — *My kitchen at Marnanie, with the John Coote armchair, upholstered in Coote & Co. Lough Eske Ivory Irish linen. The cushion is in Rose Tarlow Chablis Bay Blue.*

FOLLOWING — *The kitchen features joinery painted in my own Mount Macedon Green, limestone flooring and nickel hardware.*

Alternatively, a design narrative might emerge from a life experience that touched you somehow. The feelings and memories of that time can offer inspiration and resonate through the project. A previous home often influences the creation of a narrative. One Coote & Co. project is a case in point. When our clients' historic family home burnt down in a devastating fire, we were commissioned to work with them to redesign the interiors of the new property. We began building our narrative by researching the art and interiors of the original home: studying pictures, artefacts and books. We also asked the owners to share memories, stories and feelings from their time living in the old house. Tapping into these stories allowed us to gain a strong sense of the home's history and heritage, and thus to retain its original charm. We worked hard to create quirks and layers in the new home that would look like they had been there forever. Inspiration born of feelings and personal experiences inevitably leads to a stronger narrative.

OPPOSITE – *A vintage slipper chair reupholstered in Jim Thompson Xara Daisy beside an antique oak side table.*

ABOVE – *This beautiful door knocker was restored and reused by a client whose historic home burnt down – it was the only item rescued from the debris.*

A narrative can also be 'cold' created from something tangible or intangible. It might stem from an idea, a particular artwork, or even a rug or significant piece of furniture. For one of our Queensland projects, the client was drawn to the idea of the pineapple being a symbol of welcome. We used the pineapple motif throughout the project, replicating and reimagining it in numerous ways: we designed bespoke porcelain crockery, chose textiles and cabinetry hardware that reflected the theme, and used the iconic Coote & Co. pineapple lamp bases.

I find that spaces designed without a defined narrative can often fall down. It's not enough to fill an interior with arbitrary bits and pieces – the various elements must somehow relate to one another. An interior should tell a story. The narrative might develop over time, as new layers are introduced, but the original concept must always be kept in mind to ensure continuity and cohesiveness.

ABOVE – *Melamine tableware designed especially for our Noosa project. Outdoor Illum table from Cosh Living and Lucy dining chair from Cotswold Furniture.*

OPPOSITE (CLOCKWISE FROM TOP LEFT) – *Bespoke porcelain crockery featuring a pineapple motif; contemporary sofa upholstered in Schumacher Zebra Palm, Bragg & Co. lamp in Apple Green Crackle, cushions in Diane Bergeron Park Avenue Petite in Moss and Perennials Bubbly Sea Salt; valance in Schumacher Chevron Indoor/Outdoor Green on a bespoke Coote & Co. flat-weave rug; custom bedside tables with pineapple hardware from Chloe Alberry, Coote & Co. pineapple lamp with shade in Diane Bergeron Hudson Kelly, bedhead in Nine Muses Pineapple Kelly Green.*

Light

CHAPTER 04

Light

There are two forms of light that must be considered when designing any space: natural daylight and artificial lighting. Natural daylight should always be considered first, as it is less controllable and therefore will dictate the design of artificial lighting.

OPPOSITE — *The natural light in this entrance hallway is supplemented by pendant lights and table lamps.*

OPPOSITE & ABOVE —

*Bespoke Coote & Co. fluted glass and nickel pendant lights, manufactured
in Amsterdam, adorn this kitchen designed by Stephen Akehurst & Associates.
The joinery is painted in Resene Smoky Green.*

Working with Light

When considering the natural light in a room, or lack thereof, ask yourself the following questions. How does daylight fall in the space at different times of the day? How will the four seasons affect the movement of sunlight in the space? The answers will tell you if a room is inherently light or dark.

IF A ROOM is blessed with an abundance of natural light, then the world is your oyster. Such rooms should be designated as the primary daytime living spaces: kitchen, sitting and living areas.

If a room is naturally dark, consider whether there is a way to increase the amount of natural light.

1. **IS THERE ANYTHING** that could be changed, structurally, to increase daylight in the room?

2. **COULD YOU INCORPORATE** a mirrored wall, or hang a large mirror in the room, to increase natural light? (Mirrors are also excellent for creating the illusion of space.)

3. **IF THERE ARE** plants or structures outside that are obstructing natural light, could they be removed or relocated to increase daylight in the space?

If the answer to each of these questions is no, then it might be time to embrace the darkness and use the space for an evening room, such as a library, study or bedroom.

With a little thought, you can still create a lovely room in a space that lacks natural light. By employing some of the tips and tricks listed on the next page, a beautiful aesthetic can be achieved.

OPPOSITE – A Coote & Co. bronze sconce from our lighting manufacturer in Amsterdam, above the sink in the flower room at Marnanie.

TIPS ON LIGHTING

INCLUDE A MIXTURE of lighting types in a room. Consider wall sconces, table lamps, floor lamps, library lights and pendants. Remember: interiors, like people, look far superior by lamplight than under harsh overhead lighting.

CONSIDER INSTALLING LIGHTING at three different heights in the room: low (table lamps); medium (floor lamps or sconces); and high (hanging pendants). Create a cityscape of lighting, so to speak.

ALWAYS USE DIMMERS on sconces and pendants, to give you extra control over the atmosphere. Dimmed lights, combined with candles, can create an intimate mood for a dinner party, for example.

USE ONLY ONE type of warm-white light globe throughout. Choose halogen globes if possible, as most LEDs throw a cold bluish light, which really quashes atmosphere. (I have been known to travel with my own halogen light globes, changing hotel lamps when I arrive. My husband has a fit!)

CONSIDER WHAT A lampshade fabric will look like once it is illuminated – while a gathered red-linen lampshade might seem chic in daylight, it could look quite macabre with light shining through it.

WHERE POSSIBLE, CHOOSE lamps with the light switch on the neck of the lamp. This will save you from having to trace along the cord every time you wish to turn the light on.

IF YOU HAVE a choice, select good-quality silk electrical cords. Plastic cords can really spoil the look of a quality lamp.

CONSIDER THE SCALE of the various lights in the room. It's best to have a mixture of large and small lights, to create a sense of balance.

ASSESS THE SHAPE of each light. If it will be placed on or near something very angular – for example, on a sharp-edged square table or in front of an architectural panelled wall – choose a lamp or pendant with curves. Similarly, choose angular lamps for round tables or when positioned near soft furnishings.

DOWNLIGHTS CAN BE useful, but try not to rely on them. Design each room so it can be solely lit by lamps. A lamp-lit room looks so stylish and refined. That said, a space shouldn't be so dark you can't easily read or see around the room. And, of course, there will be times when you need to turn the downlights on – when packing a suitcase, for example.

WHEREVER YOU PLACE a chair or sofa, make sure a lamp is nearby. Likewise, bedside lights are a must. Ensure lights selected for reading by are suited to the purpose. The pool of light thrown by the lamp or sconce should be wide enough, and bright enough, to read by.

OPPOSITE – *For this project, we created a bespoke light fitting using a pair of antlers from our client's impressive collection. The oversized bronze and glass pendant light above the dining table adds to the layers of light and materiality in the space.*

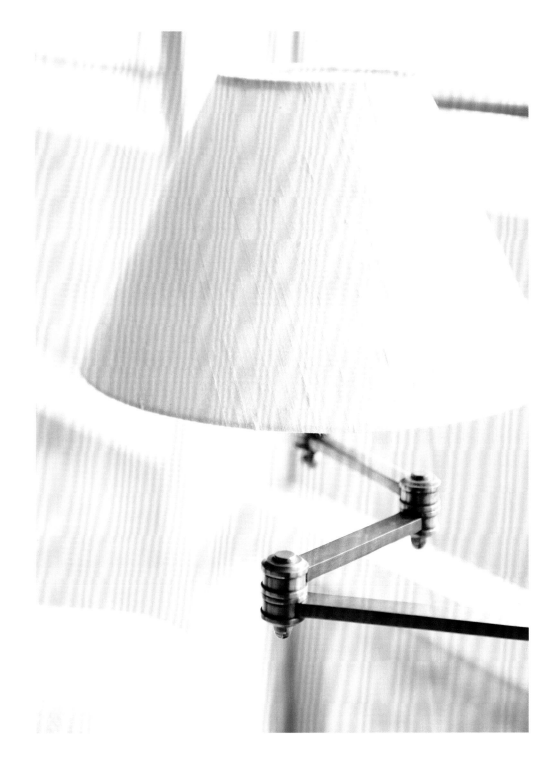

*A cityscape of lights: brass and shagreen table lamps I designed and had manufactured
in London, with box-pleated silk shades; Coote & Co. aged brass wall sconces;
and floor lamp/side table made in Amsterdam.*

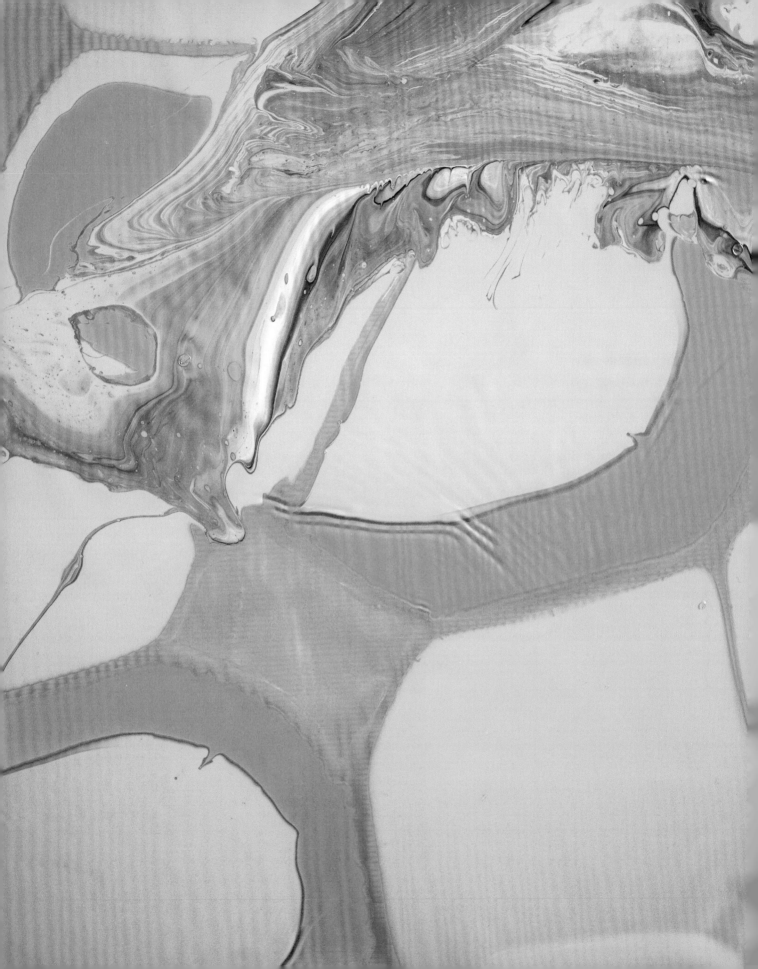

Colour

CHAPTER 05

Colour

Most people with little decorating or design experience lack confidence when working with colour. Many revert to the safety of white. While white walls and furniture can be a fabulous fresh look when done with intention, white should never be selected simply because it's the 'safe' choice. Avoiding colour out of fear of getting it wrong does not bring out the true personality of a homeowner or the authenticity of an interior. This chapter will provide you with the tools, and hopefully the confidence, to use any colour you wish in your home.

I GREW UP surrounded by colour and have always loved colour. I am constantly taking in the colours around me: the view out the window, the trees, the sky, the people walking by, the landscape I'm in. I relish using colour in my projects and find it brings life and energy to spaces. To me, colour is liveable; colour is home. I stay in rooms with minimalistic, neutral interiors from time to time when I travel, and I can appreciate them for a while – but I would never want to live in them. I use colour to add sophistication, warmth and vibrancy to my designs. Of course, used in the wrong way, colour can be vulgar and brash. There is a time and a place to show restraint and a discerning use of neutrals.

I remember my father telling me that he would often coordinate the colour scheme of an interior with the lipstick shade worn by the client – usually with great success. His knowledge and intuition when it came to colour was impressive. If I held up fifty paint samples for him to select from, he would choose the 'best' one without hesitation. If I questioned his selection – Why that specific colour and not two shades lighter, as I would have chosen? – he would explain that the obvious choice is not always the right one. Matching colours exactly was something he avoided; he found it far more interesting to create colour combinations that were slightly 'off-centre'.

OPPOSITE – *Resene Cabbage Pont on the walls in this living room makes the space feel warm and inviting, complementing the timber furniture and textile scheme.*

Ghastly good taste, it's the obviously good taste.

– after John Betjeman/Cecil Beaton

Creating a Colour Scheme

When faced with a blank canvas, it can be hard to know where to begin. Start by choosing a single hero colour for your space — the colour story will stem from there.

CHOOSING THE HERO COLOUR

1. **BEGIN WITH A** process of elimination: what colours do you like least? Understanding what you dislike is a powerful first step.

2. **TAKE NOTE OF** what you can see outside the window. Your interior should feel like it makes sense within its surroundings. Choosing a colour that complements the outdoor environment is a great way to start.

3. **CONSIDER ANY EXISTING** pieces of furniture or art that you will definitely be using in the space and draw inspiration from them.

Working with the information you have gathered, select a range of complementary colours to form the basis of your sampling options. Consider and refine this shortlist until you find your hero colour.

OPPOSITE — *In this country bedroom, walls painted in Resene Woodland are complemented by green and white textiles: Soane Tendril Vine Emerald adorns the bedhead; Nicholas Haslam Zelda Stripe Dark Green and Jane Churchill Palma Emerald feature on the cushions; and Chelsea Textiles Cupid Leaf can be seen on the lampshade. The Scottish wool throw is by Inchyra.*

THIS SPREAD – **1.** *Anna Spiro Higgledy Piggledy Stripe Green;*
2. *Colefax and Fowler Seaweed Leaf;* **3.** *Schumacher Woodperry Green;*
4. *Schumacher Promenade Indoor/Outdoor Leaf;* **5.** *Kravet Xu Garden Veridian;*
6. *Schumacher Antique Strie Velvet Olive;* **7.** *Lee Jofa Indian Zag Leaf;*
8. *Nine Muses Diamond Block Green;* **9.** *Diane Bergeron Ravello Sage Olive;*
10. *Schumacher Grand Palms Leaf;* **11.** *Holland & Sherry Grata Greenhouse;*
12. *Nina Campbell Claribel Verve;* **13.** *Rose Tarlow Glacis Juniper.*

OPPOSITE & FOLLOWING – *This conservatory, painted in a custom Porter's Paint green, is successful due to the layering of varying shades of green, which are anchored by dark metal and timber accents. Christopher Farr Cloth Ravenna can be seen on the sofas, and the windows are adorned with beautiful crewelwork curtains.*

Colour Strength

When choosing a colour, it is a good idea to select three different shades of the one colour for consideration. You can think of these as the brave, medium-brave and beige variations of your colour.

Brush each shade onto the wall and look at them in different lights. Photograph the options: invariably, you'll find the right choice will leap out at you from the images.

BRAVE

THE BOLD CHOICE. The one that will turn heads. If you get it right, it will form the foundation for a really striking interior. But if you get it wrong, it could end up looking crass, overdone or just plain ugly. (If that happens, don't fret, you can always paint over it!) The brave choice is the riskiest yet can offer the biggest rewards. It is the colour that says, 'I don't care what you think – I know what I'm doing!'

MEDIUM-BRAVE

THE CONSIDERED CHOICE. This is the colour that says, 'I know about the brave choice, but I prefer a more subtle approach. I love colour, but I want some softness and restraint.'

BEIGE

THE SAFE CHOICE. This is the colour you tend to choose when you have considered the first two options but don't trust your instincts enough to pick one of them.

OPPOSITE – *The 'brave' choice on the walls in a client's dining room: Resene Hot Chile paint and Schumacher Haruki Sisal Garnet.*

THIS SPREAD — **1.** *Namay Samay Sitaron Honey;* **2.** *Camengo Movida Camel;* **3.** *Namay Samay Lerio Golden Brown;* **4.** *Pierre Frey Ismaelia Brique Vert;* **5.** *Schumacher Prado Embroidery Saffron;* **6.** *Diane Bergeron Hudson Fabric in Copper;* **7.** *Soane Scrolling Fern Silhouette Chestnut;* **8.** *Décors Barbares Naboika Beige;* **9.** *Elliott Clarke Brussels Federal Gold;* **10.** *Colefax and Fowler Wilde Sand;* **11.** *Schumacher Isolde Stripe Yellow;* **12.** *Howe Knurl Brick;* **13.** *Soane Giraffe Diamond Gold;* **14.** *Brunschwig & Fils Jiraffa Persimmon;* **15.** *Fermoie Nut Brown Wicker;* **16.** *Soane Jajim Stripe Gold.*

TUSCANY

YULARA

FIRED EARTH

AYER'S ROCK

SOANE

OPPOSITE — *A pair of Oak Branch chandeliers by Richard Taylor hang above a custom parquetry dining table. Dining chairs upholstered in Schumacher Sinhala Linen Pomegranate.*

ABOVE — *Custom bedhead in Schumacher Campagne Rose & Ochre, with cushions in GP & J Baker Thornham Spice and custom window furnishings. The walls are painted in Resene Doeskin.*

Building a Colour Story

Once you have selected your hero colour, it is time to consider the colours you will use for your flooring and metal finishes. Whether you choose dark oak floors or pale limestone pavers will completely change the look of your scheme. Every element you put in a room adds another colour, texture and layer, so make sure you look at how all of the elements will work together.

YOU DON'T NEED to use a lot of different colours in a room to make it interesting. Using various shades of one colour can be very beautiful. Just try to ensure there is a good balance of lighter and darker elements. Colours don't need to match perfectly, but they should be complementary. You may even choose to use just a single colour and white. If you trust your instincts and make choices based on what you truly like, you'll end up with something you love – rather than something you think you *should* love.

It is perfectly fine to have different colour schemes throughout your home. The important thing is that each scheme looks like it is part of the same family story. The various colour palettes must have the same strength of character. Always consider what other rooms you can see from the room you are in: the colour schemes of each of these rooms must be good friends. A helpful way to transition colours between rooms is to have neutral hallways or common spaces. These provide visual relief and act as a bridge between different schemes.

THIS SPREAD – **1.** *Molly Mahon Dash Cotton Reverse Dark Indigo;* **2.** *Brunschwig & Fils Le Zebre Emb Navy;* **3.** *Lake August Highland Cable Marina;* **4.** *Diane Bergeron Lexington in Indigo;* **5.** *Schumacher Wilson Embroidery Indigo;* **6.** *CASA by PC Anana II Navy;* **7.** *Schumacher Aurora Damask Indigo;* **8.** *Schumacher Fiador Blue;* **9.** *Anna Spiro Grandma's Quilt Blue;* **10.** *Colefax and Fowler Wilde Blue;* **11.** *Alice Sergeant Damour Blues;* **12.** *Schumacher Kandira Sky.*

ABOVE & FOLLOWING – *The blue library at Marnanie, with Coote & Co. Gough footstool upholstered in Schumacher Fishnet Marine; sofa upholstery in Georgia Macmillan Double Inky Stripe; cushions in Schumacher Mariga Delft; Carleton V Safari Sky on lampshades and cushions. Artwork by The Winsome Collection (Lantern print),* The Promise of Life, c. 1890. *Walls painted in Resene Nauti.*

OPPOSITE – *Walls in Porters Paints Whale Watching provide the backdrop to a bedhead in Schumacher Arroyo Stripe Indigo and cushion in Schumacher Zonda Indigo. Coote & Co. natural pineapple lamp, with shade in Nicholas Haslam Hampton Stripe Navy on White.*

Sampling Paint Colours

A 'brush-out' is imperative when it comes to finalising your paint colour choices.

BRUSH OUT SAMPLE paint colours on the walls of the actual room you are decorating, and fill at least 1 square metre (10 square feet) – don't be stingy!

BRUSH OUT COLOURS in different areas of the house to see how they look and how they make you feel in each space.

LIGHT HAS A huge impact on the way colour looks in a room. Observe your sample colours at different times of day and with varying lighting.

BRUSH-OUTS CAN be a great way to communicate to clients or family members what you are trying to create and achieve.

If you undertake extensive sampling, you're almost certain to end up with the result you want. However, like any of us, you might not always get things right. Have the confidence to call out a colour mistake and rectify it (preferably quickly). Don't worry what the upholsterer, painter or builder might think – you have to live with your project for much longer than they will. As you gain experience over time, mistakes will become less and less frequent.

*OPPOSITE – **1.** Cloth & Clover The Littletons Rhubarb; **2.** Sarah Hardaker Coco Faded Red; **3.** Kelly Wearstler Graffito Salmon/Cream; **4.** Nicole Fabre Beaucaire Persian Pink; **5.** Mimi Pickard Pebble Pink; **6.** Bennison Fabrics Dragon Flower Pink Green on Oyster; **7.** John Robshaw Shali Lotus; **8.** Namay Samay Zeimoto Raspberry; **9.** Anna Spiro Camona Heirloom Pink/ Taupe/Mustard; **10.** Nina Campbell Poquelin Mourlot Velvet; **11.** Namay Samay Zeimoto Frangipani; **12.** John Stefanidis Pelargonium Salmon; **13.** Bennison Fabrics Roses Shocking Pink on Oyster; **14.** Colefax and Fowler Seafern Red.*

*My daughter Daphne's bedroom: Resene Cosmos on the walls pairs beautifully with
the slightly clashing pink of the Kathryn Ireland toile used for the beds and curtains.*

A Pink Story

When we bought Marnanie, the dining room was painted white.
However, my friend John Graham informed me that when he owned
the property, the room had been painted rhododendron pink. Back then
(some forty years ago), my father had made pink and white John Stefanidis
cotton curtains for the room. Luckily for me, the curtains were still there,
and they formed the beginning of my colour narrative. I decided to restore
the curtains and create my own version of the pink dining room, inspired
by the pink rhododendrons in the garden.

THE NEW WALL colour was definitely a 'brave' choice: a bright high-gloss rhododendron pink. But I felt the room could take it, since it was small and intimate. Originally, I only painted above the dado rail, but I thought the room needed more – so I painted below the dado rail. Finally, I realised I had to commit completely, so I painted the ceiling pink as well. It was all or nothing.

With such a strong wall colour, it was imperative that I carefully balance the various other elements in the room to avoid the whole thing looking like a lolly box. For the dining chair fabric, I selected a mid-scale print featuring greens and blues, with a hint of pink. The diverse, soft colours of the fabric, along with the scale of the print, helped to offset the boldness of the pink walls and provide visual relief. A small-scale print could have looked almost like another solid colour, whereas the mid-scale print brought a sense of movement and life.

To add a touch of glamour to the room, I designed a copper and crystal chandelier – the tone of the copper complemented the pink nicely, while offering a more subtle look than brass. Then I hung a large artwork by Indigenous artist Kathleen Ngale to provide texture and further variations of pink. Finally, to create contrast and anchor the room, I installed neutral sisal flooring and chose a dark hardwood pedestal dining table – without them the room would have been *too* pretty.

OPPOSITE & FOLLOWING –

The pink dining room at Marnanie, painted in high-gloss Resene Glamour Puss. The chandelier, which features copper leaves and hand-cut Italian crystal, was manufactured in London.

The curtains, in a pink John Stefanidis textile, were originally installed by my father for Kevin O'Neill and John Graham. I restored them by removing the tattered edges and adding a new pink linen base-band.

WHITE FLAG

PROVENCE BLUE

JODPHUR BLUE

ANTIQUE BLUE

CURRARONG (AGNSW)

BREAK

NAPOLEO

HAMPTON'S BL

TIPS ON PAINT COLOUR

IF A ROOM is naturally light, keep it that way by using light paint colours.

IF A ROOM is naturally dark, and no amount of restructuring can change this fact, embrace it – paint the room to make it even darker.

YOU CAN SOMETIMES get away with painting a light room dark, but you can never get away with painting a dark room light.

THE CEILING OF a room always needs to be lighter than the walls. This gives the illusion of a higher ceiling and hence more space, which one usually wants to achieve. Use a half-strength version of your wall colour, or white.

UNDERSTAND THE WHITES: cool whites have a blue-grey undertone and are better suited to coastal and contemporary interiors; warm whites have a cream undertone and are better suited to country and classic interiors.

VERY SMALL ROOMS can often take a lot of colour, while very large rooms are more suited to lighter shades.

IF A ROOM starts to look either too full of colour or too white, this can be countered by adding a dark element (such as a dark-coloured table or sofa) to anchor the space.

WHEN CHOOSING A wall paint for a beach house or rural property, consider the colours of the environment outside. Tree barks, for example, exhibit some beautiful tonal combinations. Often, the answer lies in those shades.

OPPOSITE – *1. Barneby Gates Artichoke Thistle; 2. Kelly Wearstler Graffito Teal/Pearl; 3. Nicole Fabre Vaison Bleu Anglais; 4. Lewis & Wood Berry Brothers Delft; 5. Nicholas Haslam Bamboo Cane Blue on White; 6. Chelsea Textiles Stars in Blue and Galaxy in Indigo; 7. Phillip Jeffries Manila Hemp Navy; 8. Rose Tarlow Velours Cord Baltic; 9. Schumacher Linen Stripe Sky; 10. Rose Tarlow Glacis Nori; 11. Kelly Wearstler Avant Sky Teal; 12. Colefax and Fowler Panthera Old Blue; 13. Nicole Fabre Bukhara Indigo; 14. Rose Tarlow Chablis Bay Blue/Natural.*

Resene Green Meets Blue on the walls of this country bedroom is contrasted and layered with Soane Scrolling Fern Azure on the bedhead. The client's vintage textile has been used for the bed cushions, alongside Soane Old Flax Sky Blue.

Neutrals & White Are Colours Too

White is fabulous when used in the right way and in the right place. I am a huge fan of British interior decorator Syrie Maugham and her all-white interiors. In the 1920s and 30s, she was a trailblazer, layering all shades and textures of white and neutrals to create an incredibly sophisticated look. However, if white is to be used, it must be because it is the best choice for the interior — not the safe choice. To properly execute a neutral interior, you must achieve a depth of texture and materiality.

WHEN PAINTING WALLS white, I often lean towards a warm white. It is more soft and inviting, and easier to live with. Be careful your warm whites are not too yellow, though, as whites like this will date.

A NOTE ON WHITES — Some of my go-to warm whites are Popcorn and Eggshell by Porter's Paints; Natural White and Hog Bristle by Dulux; and Bianca, Half Bianca and Quarter Fossil by Resene.

Good cool white options include Lexicon, White on White and Casper White by Dulux; Alpen by Porter's Paints; and Black White and Alabaster by Resene.

OPPOSITE — 1. Schumacher Vento Embroidery Natural; 2. Nina Campbell Bagatelle Weave Beige/Ivory; 3. International Floor Coverings Manzanilla 2 Tone (Pearl-Malay) Abaca; 4. Kelly Wearstler Graffito Ii Ivory/Ebony; 5. Pintura Studio Caspian Chalk/Coffee; 6. Schumacher Mohave Natural; 7. Cadrys Boheme Ribbed Tan; 8. Colefax and Fowler Panthera Chocolate; 9. Leffler Aniline Tan and Fawn; 10. Coote & Co. Bellamont Forest Ivory.

PALE CLAY

MUDLARK

WET CEMENT

SHALE

OPPOSITE & ABOVE – *Stone, timber, bone, linen and silver give depth and interest to these spaces.*

FOLLOWING – *Contemporary artwork by Robert Doble adds rich neutrals to this room.*

Textiles

CHAPTER 06

Textiles

Textiles are an essential part of any interior. Whether used for furniture upholstery, cushion covers, curtains or rugs, the colours, textures and patterns of textiles bring interest and depth to a room. However, using textiles to maximum effect requires a degree of confidence and understanding.

MY RELATIONSHIP WITH textiles has been quite a journey. Although I feel I have always had an innate understanding of textiles, in the early days of my career I definitely lacked confidence when using them. By continuing to work with textiles over many years, and undertaking extensive research, I have educated my eye and gradually built up my skill and confidence. With the right amount of interest, patience and passion, this is something anyone can do.

OPPOSITE — *Contrasting textures and patterns make for a rich textile scheme. Here, Colefax and Fowler Eaton Check Fawn covers our John Coote armchair, with cushions in Larsen Barragan Ebony and Jim Thompson Xara Daisy. The Boheme rug is from Cadrys.*

Creating a Textile Scheme

When creating a textile scheme, a good starting point is to choose one hero textile, from which the rest of the scheme will develop. This first textile could be simply a fabric you really love, a vintage textile, or a textile you've found that perfectly corresponds to an artwork or rug that you know will be used in the room. Once you've selected your hero textile, you can begin to build additional textiles into the scheme.

TO CREATE COHESION and harmony in your scheme, consider the following types of textiles and how they can be used to balance each other. Keep in mind that these principles apply not only to fabrics and upholstery but also to floor coverings such as rugs and carpet.

LARGE-SCALE PATTERNS

The motif is big and only repeats across the width of the fabric two or three times. If patterns will form part of your scheme, select this textile first. Best used for larger items, so that the whole pattern is visible.

SMALL-SCALE PATTERNS

The pattern repeat is petite and covers the fabric many times over. Can be used to offset a larger-scale print.

REPETITIVE PATTERNS

The shape featured on the print repeats consistently. Examples include spots, lozenges, stars, stripes, circles and squares. Can be used to anchor an unruly or organic pattern.

STRUCTURED PATTERNS

The pattern is more lineal – examples include checks, stripes, ticking and geometric patterns. Can be used to ground an organic print.

ORGANIC PATTERNS

The pattern is less structured, often with no beginning or end, no rhyme or rhythm. The print may be wild or whimsical, like a floral or rambling garden story. Can add drama and an element of disorganisation to a scheme.

PLAIN TEXTILES

A plain colour with no pattern or motif at all. Can be used to balance any pattern or anchor a busy scheme.

The most important thing to understand when balancing a textile scheme is that opposites attract. So, where you have used a large-scale print, be sure to add a small-scale one. Where you have used a structured pattern, balance it with an organic one. In addition, try to ensure a common thread runs through your entire scheme: for example, all the textiles may share the same colour palette.

OPPOSITE – This bedroom, designed for a little girl, features a beautiful blue toile, Kumo Village Sky by Schumacher, on the bedhead and cushions. We added layers of contrasting blue in the curtain bands and the Coote & Co. Marnanie rug.

OPPOSITE, ABOVE & FOLLOWING —

A combination of patterned textiles can be seen in this room: large-scale (armchairs), small-scale (cushions and gathered lampshades), structured (ottoman and sofa) and organic (cushions). The scheme started with the Susan Deliss fabric on the ottoman. Complementary and clashing blue, red and neutral textiles with differing textures complete the scheme.

CLOCKWISE FROM TOP LEFT — *Lincoln Brooks Pretzel chair upholstered in Janus et Cie Annabel Porcelain with blue piping; Manuel Canovas Texas Ciel with Coote & Co. Baronscourt Irish linen in Billow and Schumacher Teton Snow; sofa upholstered in Nina Campbell Rodmell Aqua with cushions in Colefax and Fowler Appledore Check Beige and Lewis & Wood Daisy Chintz, and Coote & Co. custom rug; cushions in Colefax and Fowler Casimir Old Blue, Kathryn M Ireland Ikat Check Blue and Inchyra Beaumont Check Sage.*

CLOCKWISE FROM TOP LEFT — *Bedhead in Schumacher Chevron Indoor/Outdoor Green, cushion with Diane Bergeron Park Avenue Petite Moss; Brunschwig & Fils Bird and Thistle Blue wallpaper, with custom embroidered scalloped sham; Coote & Co. Andrea slipper chair upholstered in Schumacher Iconic Leopard Green on flat-weave geometric rug; Colefax and Fowler Kendal Leaf Green bed drapes trimmed in Diane Bergeron Grosgrain Ribbon Sage rest on bespoke Coote & Co. flat-weave lozenge rug.*

OPPOSITE — *Resene Cooled Green walls make for a serene bedroom. Bed chair upholstered in Inchyra Beaumont Check Wool Sage, with curtains in Coote & Co. Lough Eske Ivory Irish linen. Bespoke, hand-carved pineapple finials are on all the curtain rods at Marnanie.*

CLOCKWISE FROM TOP LEFT — *Cushion in Nicholas Haslam Zelda Stripe Dark Green rests on a Soane Seaweed Lace Emerald window seat; a fabric trio of Schumacher Fishnet Marine, Schumacher Mariga Delft and Carleton V Safari Sky; chair in Rose Tarlow Glacis Chard with Rose Tarlow Chablis Bay Blue cushion; bespoke Coote & Co. flat-weave lozenge rug.*

Types of Textile Scheme

THE HERO TEXTILE SCHEME

OFTEN THE EASIEST and most successful schemes begin with a single hero textile. The hero textile must be a fabric that speaks to you, whether because of its particular colour, pattern or scale, and it must also make sense in the room you are using it in. This one really fabulous textile becomes the centrepiece of the space. The rest of the scheme builds on and supports this foundation.

THE SINGULAR TEXTILE SCHEME

YOU DON'T ALWAYS have to work with several different textiles in a room. Sometimes it can be interesting to pick a single textile and simply cover everything in it. Seeing one superb textile en masse can be really striking. This type of scheme always reminds me of the 1980s, particularly the bedroom I had as a little girl, with that beautiful pink chintz on the bed, curtains and wallpaper.

If you are tempted to try this style, it is important to modernise or reinvent the look, as otherwise it can appear dated. To help bring it into the 21st century, add some contemporary art or furniture with a contrasting colour or finish, or incorporate a plain fabric to provide relief from the main textile.

THE MONOCHROMATIC SCHEME

STICKING TO A single colour within a room can have a strong visual impact and really make a statement. A palette based on a single colour will only work if you use many layers: using six or seven shades of the chosen colour will create depth, interest and sophistication. It can look even better if a few of those shades clash. The same principle applies when creating an entirely white or neutral room – it will work best if many shades of white/neutrals are layered together. If all the elements in a scheme match too much, the room can end up looking flat or contrived.

OPPOSITE – *For my bedroom at Marnanie I used Colefax and Fowler Kendal Leaf Green on the bedhead, four-poster drapes, lampshades, day bed and armchair. It is a fresh and whimsical print which has a great visual impact when used en masse.*

OPPOSITE – *A balanced textile scheme: the hero textile here is Nine Muses Pineapple Kelly; the small-scale print on the lampshade is Diane Bergeron Hudson Kelly; a structured pattern can be seen in the bespoke Coote & Co. rug, while the cushions add layers of texture.*

ABOVE – *The design of this room centres on the curved bedhead, upholstered in striking Texas Ciel by Manuel Canovas. The cushions, drapes, rug and throw all complement this feature with their texture and subtlety.*

Understanding Texture

If you are aiming for a more layered look, be sure to consider the diversity of textures in your scheme. To create interest and depth in a room, try using a combination of materials: linen, silk, cotton and wool. Each fabric will reflect light differently and feel different to the touch. Using a range of textures is particularly important if you are creating a monochromatic colour scheme.

ABOVE — *Contrasting textures: velvet and delicate embroidered linen.*

OPPOSITE — *Everything has a texture. Here, gilt objects, bricks, sheer curtains, textured artwork, velvet upholstery, painted timber and woollen carpet come together to create a rich and interesting room.*

OPPOSITE & ABOVE —

This scheme is made rich by the numerous shades of green and varying textures of linen,
velvet, embroidery and crewelwork.

Sampling Textiles

It is essential to see samples of your textiles in real life – images online are never an accurate representation of how the fabric will actually look. Ensure you lay out all of your textile samples next to each other to make sure they work well together. Although you may have only a small piece of each textile, try to imagine how much visual space each will command in your finished room. You might decide to use a particular fabric to cover just one small cushion, while another might be used to upholster a large sofa.

OPPOSITE – *When choosing textiles, don't forget about white. In a bedroom, white sheets can contrast nicely with colourful or detailed elements. To soften a large expanse of white bed linen, layer with a throw, blankets or vintage quilts. Here, the walls are Resene Casal and the bedhead is in Colefax and Fowler Perdita Antique Blue.*

TIPS ON TEXTILES

BE CONFIDENT IN your own taste. You may admire the work of designers who create intricate, layered textile schemes, combining fifteen patterns in one room. Or you may prefer a far more simple, liveable style. Stick with what you love and know, and you can't go wrong.

PRINTS ARE MORE forgiving than plains: they can be less conspicuous than a solid-colour fabric and are a lot more durable, as they don't show wear as much. A print, rather than a plain fabric, would be the practical choice for the sofa of a family with young children and pets, for example.

WHEN CHOOSING A fabric, consider the strength and thickness required for its intended purpose, taking into account how often the item will be used. The type of material (wool, cotton, silk, linen) is also important.

DON'T USE 100 PER CENT linen for roman blinds, as they will soon lose their shape. Instead, go for a cotton–linen blend, which offers more structure.

IF YOU HAVE a rug you are planning to use in a room, take it as the starting point from which to build your scheme. Is the pattern organic or structured? What is its texture like? And therefore, what other textiles will you need to use to create a balanced scheme?

IF YOU ARE having difficulty finalising a scheme, take a photograph of all the textile samples together. Wait a day, then look at the image – it will reveal exactly what you need to do to balance the scheme.

OPPOSITE – The hero of this room is the beautiful curved bedhead in Schumacher Grand Palms Leaf. This print is balanced by Linen Stripe wallpaper in Blush and complemented by the small-scale Folly Temple on the cushions, both by Schumacher. Pintura Studio's Caspian Granny Apple/Sapphire on the lampshade adds another layer of green. Day bed in Osborne & Little Colby Blush.

Furniture Layout

CHAPTER 07

Furniture Layout

Rooms designed to enhance conversation, comfort and functionality are, to me, the most successful. In a space that is comfortable and considered, you don't have to shout to be heard by the person sitting opposite at the dinner table, or get up from your armchair to set down a drink or book.

WHEN DECIDING HOW the furniture in a room will be arranged, it is important to consider all the different ways the space could be laid out. Compare the various options, and weigh the problems and advantages of each. Often the best solution will be a combination of one or more of your potential layouts.

By following some simple guidelines, the most fitting layout will soon reveal itself.

OPPOSITE — *I designed this custom console to balance the large scale of this entrance hall.*

ABOVE — *Diane Bergeron's Babe ottoman, upholstered in a Kravet check, stands on Tuscan Arezzo Sisal by International Floor Coverings.*

Furnish your room for conversation and the chairs will take care of themselves.

– Sibyl Colefax

Creating a Floor Plan

When designing the layout of any room, it is essential to create a scale floor plan. This plan shows the exact dimensions of the room, and the placement and size of each element you will include. If you don't have the skills to draw up a plan yourself, enlist the help of a designer, draftsperson or architect. An accurate floor plan will allow you to check your proposed layout for functionality and flow. For example, you can easily measure whether walkways are wide enough, or whether there is ample space for dining chairs to be pushed in and out. A floor plan may need to be revised many times before you arrive at your final layout.

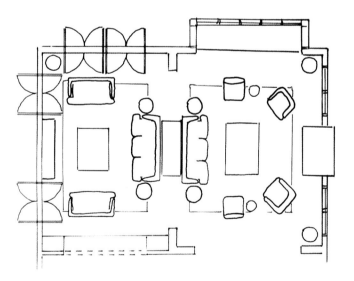

OPPOSITE – *A scale floor plan was essential in the successful design of this space, as I had to work with several entrance points while maximising seating and allowing for easy movement through the room.*

ABOVE & FOLLOWING – *Splitting this large living area into two 'rooms' was the best way to maximise functionality in this client's space. Two rugs and back-to-back sofas visually divide the area, along with a narrow table in between. Rugs are a wonderful way to create rooms within rooms.*

Creating a Great Focal Point

*The focal point of your room should be
a central item or asset, like a fabulous
big rug, a beautiful fireplace, a striking
artwork or even a spectacular view.
Choose your focal point first, then build
the layout of the room around it. Begin
by looking at the architecture of the space
and then consider which pieces you will
use to fill it.*

OPPOSITE — *The focal point for this room was the beautiful
fireplace: I designed built-in bookshelves to go on either side
of it, and positioned furniture so that people could comfortably
sit, chat and have a drink around the fire.*

Creating Balance & Symmetry

It is important to create balance and symmetry in your layout. The various pieces of furniture must work together harmoniously. To achieve balance, follow the 'opposites attract' principle: combine furniture that is big and small, curved and straight, tall and short, hard and upholstered, old and new, or masculine and feminine. (Chapter 9 goes into more detail on using opposites.) To create symmetry, place similar or matching pieces opposite each other in the space (try this with chairs, side tables and lamps).

THE EYE SHOULD be drawn around the entire room, not to one element in particular. If one piece is standing out too much, it may be an indication that the layout is not balanced. Conversely, if a certain component is getting lost among the scheme, you may need to try rearranging things.

OPPOSITE – *Pairs and opposites play a big role in creating balance in this space: the pair of upholstered sofas is balanced by the pair of timber pretzel chairs; the pair of prints is balanced by the sculptural table with model boat; and the abaca rug is softened by the Charolais hide.*

FOLLOWING – *The Marnanie kitchen is designed so that the fireplace and glass-fronted cupboards occupy the same space, visually, as the pantry and integrated fridge on the opposite side. The timber dining table, positioned at one end of the room, is balanced by a Welsh oak dresser at the other end.*

TIPS ON FURNITURE LAYOUT

Below are some of my golden rules for furniture layout. However, remember that in design, as in life, some rules are meant to be broken. If you do decide to break the rules: never complain, and never ever explain.

ENSURE THAT AMPLE walkways are included in each room and that they are not too narrow. A main thoroughfare through any given room (e.g. between the back of an armchair and the wall) should be a minimum of 80 centimetres (30 inches) wide.

A BIG ROOM can often work well with less furniture, while a small room is more appealing when it has lots of furniture.

EVERY SEAT IN a room should have a table within arm's reach.

ALL CHAIRS – WHETHER armchair, dining chair, breakfast-bar stool, or sofa – must be inviting and comfortable.

IN LIVING AND dining spaces, there should be enough chairs to accommodate the home's residents, plus additional seating that can be utilised for guests.

OCCASIONAL CHAIRS, WHICH are light and easy to move, are a good option for extra seating. Placed symmetrically around the perimeter of a room, they can be a feature of interest until needed.

AVOID PLACING SOFAS in front of floor-to-ceiling windows, as they will block out too much light.

RUGS SHOULD BE positioned at least 40 centimetres (16 inches) away from walls, and away from solid pieces of furniture like television consoles and book cases. Ensure the front legs (at least) of your sofa or armchair stand on the rug.

DESIGN ANY BUILT-IN joinery – wardrobes, cabinetry and shelving – to be as tall as possible. Not only will this provide more storage space, but it will make the ceiling feel higher by drawing the eye upwards.

FREESTANDING FURNITURE CAN be more interesting and storied than built-in joinery. If you can't find a piece that is quite the right size, you can make it appear larger by flanking it with a pair of chairs.

CHOOSE BEDSIDE TABLES that are as large as will fit in the room, to provide plenty of space for lamps, books, reading glasses, cups of tea and vases of flowers.

OPPOSITE – *My daughter Sybil's room, with The Countess wallpaper by Charlotte Gaisford, custom bedhead in Coote & Co. Baronscourt Irish linen Billow, and Coote & Co. pineapple lamp base.*

Repurposing

CHAPTER 08

Repurposing

If an item is of high quality when it is purchased, it will likely remain in good condition for many decades to come. Fast interiors, like fast fashion, are not sustainable. It's easy to be tempted by trendy, inexpensive furnishings, but these tend to date quickly and are usually poorly made. They generally need replacing before too long. Cheap furniture is costly to the environment, to your aesthetic and, in the long run, to your pocket.

OPPOSITE & ABOVE —

This timeless and beautiful chair was discovered in the house of our client's grandmother. Re-covered with Tendril Vine from Soane, it was installed in the new property, ready for its next stage in life.

Repurposing Antiques

A good way to save money and add charm to your interiors is by repurposing quality antiques. I often encourage my clients to take a second look at inherited items they may consider dated or drab – a set of Georgian dining chairs from their grandmother, for example. With a little imagination and resourcefulness – a splash of paint or an exciting new textile – pieces like these can be given a second life. Sentimental value shouldn't be overlooked. Family heirlooms can add a real sense of character and history to a room.

INHERITING INTERESTING, GOOD-QUALITY pieces is wonderful, but of course it's not the only way to source antiques. Search markets, antique shops and auction houses, as well as online marketplaces like *Invaluable* and *1stDibs*, to find remarkable items from around the world. Through experience, you will educate your eye, and certain items will begin to pop out at you – these are the pieces that will make your interiors sing.

I recently bought a pair of beautiful English Georgian silver-plated shell sconces from a dealer in New York. I installed them in my powder room to add history, glamour and a further layer of materiality.

ABOVE & OPPOSITE –

Reupholstering these 1940s hand-sprung chairs in Bamboo Trellis, a smart Paolo Moschino textile, and re-staining the frames transformed them from tired to sophisticated.

OPPOSITE – *A fresh Fermoie shade in Nut Brown Wicker gave this turn-of-the-century lamp a new lease of life.*

ABOVE – *Magic happens in the workroom of one of Coote & Co.'s skilled upholsterers, CW Howell Upholstery.*

Buying New

Quality doesn't often come cheap, but purchasing furniture for your interiors shouldn't break the bank. It's a matter of prioritising. Choose carefully and invest in specific, good-quality, timeless pieces that can stay with you through many years, or as you move from home to home. The real beauty of good-quality furniture is that it can be repurposed and restored ad infinitum.

A GREAT-QUALITY hand-sprung sofa, for example, should serve you for a lifetime. After your children, pets or red-wine-drinking friends have pushed the sofa to its limits, simply reimagine it back to life. Reupholster it in a beautiful textile, perhaps changing the details with contrast piping, buttoning or fringing, and add some gorgeous new cushions. Restoring a piece of furniture you already own is far more sustainable and economical than replacing it with something new.

OPPOSITE – *I designed this oversized sofa for a client with young children and a dog. The Schumacher Zonda Indoor/Outdoor textile in Indigo is fun, contemporary and will be forgiving on stains. The sofa itself is handmade and high quality, and will last for decades to come.*

ABOVE – *Upholstery details of a bedroom chair in Kravet Xu Garden Veridian.*

Recently, while working on a large country property, I discovered a set of beautiful chintz curtains from yesteryear. They were frail and faded along the edges, where the sun had damaged them. However, the colour, quality and detail of the fabric was exquisite. The print was unique, depicting a whimsical garden scene of botanical motifs and peacocks in greens, teals and blues.

As only small pieces were in adequate condition, the fabric was used for bed and sofa cushions, and an occasional chair. This textile informed the schemes for all four bedrooms, elegantly tying in with the garden setting of the local landscape.

English Georgian silver-plated shell sconces bring the powder room to life,
adding history and a layer of materiality.

Miss Wightman's Wingback Chair

*Miss Lillian Wightman, who founded the iconic fashion house
Le Louvre in Melbourne in the 1920s, once gifted my father a beautiful
wingback leather armchair. He cherished the chair so much he had it
transported from Australia to his house in Ireland.*

THE CHAIR, WITH its worn tan-green waxed leather, was perfectly proportioned for my dad. It took pride of place in his study, where he often sat to work. After Dad died, in 2012, my siblings and I shipped the chair back to Melbourne and returned it to Miss Wightman's daughter, Georgina Weir, who now owns Le Louvre. Georgina re-covered parts of the chair that were damaged in fabulous Scottish tartans. And so the chair lives anew.

ABOVE & OPPOSITE —

*The wingback armchair: in Dad's study in Ireland (above); and (opposite), having been returned
to its first family, in Georgina Weir's sitting room in Australia.*

The Georgian Console

While living in Ireland, I co-designed a Georgian-style console for our then home, Bellamont Forest. We created the table based on a sketch by Sir Edward Lovett Pearce, the architect of the estate, which we found in the library archives. We used mahogany for the base and sourced marble from a local County Kilkenny quarry for the tabletop. International artisans were enlisted to manufacture the piece to our precise specifications.

UNFORTUNATELY, AT SOME point over the years, the console's central shell motif was broken after suffering a hard knock. Although it was carefully restored, the joins remained visible – to me, this just added to its character. I was lucky to inherit the piece when my father died. I shipped it back to Australia and had the base hand-painted white in gesso. The console now stands in the bay window of my sitting room at Marnanie, a much loved and storied piece.

Sir Edward Lovett Pearce's original sketch of the console.

OPPOSITE & RIGHT – *The Georgian console in the sitting room at Marnanie, and at Bellamont Forest in Ireland (right).*

Opposites Attract

CHAPTER 09

Opposites Attract

Using juxtaposition and contrast really appeals to me, as it is such an effective way of creating balance in a design. Employing 'opposites' in a scheme, or within any collection or group of items, can help create equilibrium. Imagine a beautiful stone floor layered with a natural sisal rug, a marble coffee table next to a comfortable linen sofa, or a white bust in front of a dark wall. The principle of creating balance with contrasting or opposite elements is used in many creative processes, including cooking, garden design, art and fashion.

IT'S IMPORTANT TO understand that just because two things are 'opposite' doesn't mean they can't have certain qualities in common. A mantelpiece collection of objects made from a range of materials such as glass, metal and porcelain could look a bit of a mess; but if the pieces all share the same colour palette, they can form a cohesive and aesthetically pleasing group. Opposites with a common thread make for rich and interesting interiors.

As a tool, the 'opposites attract' concept can be adapted to solve a visual problem or improve an overall aesthetic. In this chapter, I outline a number of ways you can use opposites to create balance and harmony in your interiors.

OPPOSITE — *The sitting room at Marnanie is full of opposites that create balance: a high-gloss modern side table next to an antique turned-leg footstool; an English-style armchair with fringing beside a contemporary minimalist sofa; a distressed antique rug over natural sisal flooring.*

FOLLOWING — *The whimsical pattern of Colefax and Fowler Kendal Leaf is balanced by the structure of the Coote & Co. flat-weave rug and the bamboo sofa's natural texture. Blue walls provide a bold contrast, with pops of white from curtains and artworks delivering moments of relief.*

Using Opposites to Create Balance

MATERIALITY

IN INTERIOR DESIGN, materiality refers to the materials or base elements used in a space: stone, wood, tile, textiles, etc. Consider the mix of textures in your interior. Try to balance materials that are rough to the touch, such as unfinished stone or wood, with others that are smooth and perhaps luxurious, such as polished marble or delicate fabric.

PERIOD

COMBINING FURNITURE, TEXTILES, lighting and art from different eras creates depth and balance. Try mixing mid-century lights, mirrors and sculptures with 18th-century furniture, for example.

SCALE

I OFTEN UPSCALE sofas and armchairs when I have them manufactured. I find my clients like the comfort of oversized seating. However, it is important to balance larger items like these with smaller pieces of furniture, such as occasional chairs and side tables.

EXPENSE

WHEN SOURCING FURNISHINGS and art, your first consideration should be the aesthetic appeal of the item and how it could enhance your space. The expense of a piece should never dictate its perceived value or appeal. If you find beauty in a vintage cane sofa that costs $10, listen to your gut and buy it. Trust your instincts. Naturally, it is important at times to invest in more expensive art and furnishings. A combination of high-quality and affordable pieces will create balance and bring credibility to a scheme. Don't be afraid to mix expensive items with inexpensive ones, as long as they all resonate with you.

OPPOSITE – *The kitchen chairs at Marnanie feature loose Irish linen covers. The soft, natural fibre balances the solid limestone flagstones used for the floor. While the textures of the two materials are opposite, the colours relate.*

MASCULINE AND FEMININE

MANY OF THE elements that make up an interior can be thought of as having a distinctly masculine or feminine quality. Pieces that have a hard texture, large size, dark colour or straight outlines might be considered masculine. Conversely, pieces that have a soft texture, smaller size, curved lines or a pretty silhouette might be considered feminine. Within any room, there should be a balance of masculine and feminine.

Even if you are designing a traditionally masculine space – a hearty country gentleman's study, perhaps – consider including a more elegant piece to create balance.

COLOUR

CONTRAST IS VERY important when creating textile and colour schemes: there should always be a balance between light and dark colours. A pop of black in an all-white interior can create visual interest and variety. Strong or bright colours can be balanced with softer, more neutral tones.

ORIGIN

COMBINING FURNISHINGS FROM different regions can make for an interesting look. Try mixing European furniture with Asian sculptures and textiles, for example. Edit and curate along the way, to ensure there is a sense of cohesion. An interior in which every item looks as if it has come from a single shop, or a single country, will inevitably appear dull or uninspired.

SHAPE

IT IS ALSO important to curate and balance differing shapes. A room with too many curves can come across as hectic, while one with too many straight lines can look harsh or cold.

OPPOSITE – *Green and pink, white and timber, patterned and plain, curved and straight – this mix shows how well opposites can create balance.*

ABOVE – *The breakfast area at this Portsea residence is full of colour, texture and light.*
The sculptural and highly textured fossilised travertine table base is softened by the upholstered slipper
chairs in Georgia Macmillan Indigo Spot. The vase is from Carolina Irving & Daughters.

OPPOSITE – *The palette for this study was inspired by our clients' collection of artworks.*
Bold Resene Cupid walls contrast with the colour and design of the armchair's Temple fabric by
Nicholas Haslam and the pale-green striped curtains. A writing desk from Graham Geddes Antiques
and a classic brass and timber lamp ground the vibrant colour scheme.

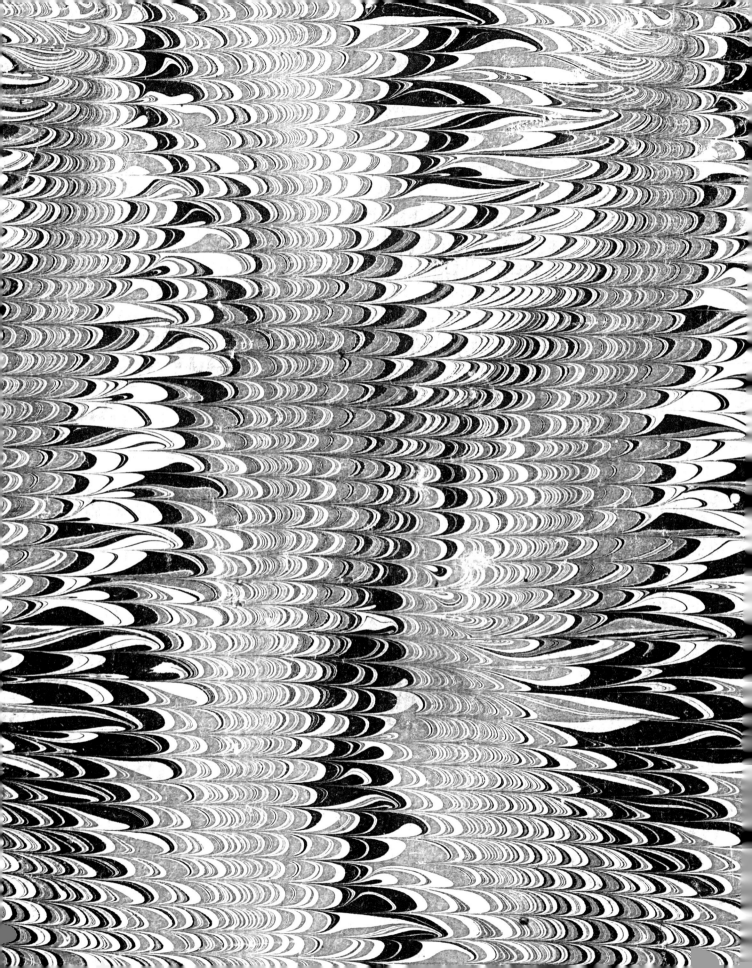

Favourite Books

CHAPTER 10

Favourite Books

Here, I share some of the books that have influenced me the most, and which I continue to reference often when commencing new projects.

WHEN READING A design book, it should be with the intent of educating your eye. Read the entire book, study every photograph, digest the finer details. Try to understand why and how the designer creates the way they do, even if the aesthetic doesn't necessarily align with your own tastes. Let their ideas and methods inspire your creative process.

CLASSIC CONTEMPORARY
INTERIORS & DESIGN

*Nina Campbell: Interior Decoration –
Elegance and Ease*, by Giles Kime

*English Decoration: Timeless Inspiration
for the Contemporary Home*, by Ben Pentreath

Blue and White and Other Colour Stories,
by William Yeoward

David Hicks: Designer, by Ashley Hicks

Axel Vervoordt: Timeless Interiors, by Armelle Baron

Veere Grenney: A Point of View: On Decorating,
by Veere Grenney

*Colefax and Fowler: The Best in English Interior
Decoration*, by Chester Jones

Beautiful: All-American Decorating and Timeless Style,
by Mark D Sykes

More Beautiful: All-American Decoration,
by Mark D Sykes

Robert Kime, by Alastair Langlands

Beata Heuman: Every Room Should Sing,
by Beata Heuman

*Inspirational Interiors: Classic English Interiors from
Colefax and Fowler*, by Roger Banks-Pye

The Interiors of Chester Jones, by Henry Russell

CLASSIC & CONTEMPORARY
FURNITURE HISTORY

Eileen Gray: Her Life and Work, by Peter Adam

Chairs: A History, by Florence de Dampierre

The Gentleman and Cabinet-Maker's Director,
by Thomas Chippendale (published 1754)

Irish Furniture, by The Knight of Glin and James Peill

BEAUTIFUL HOMES
& LIFESTYLE

*One Man's Folly: The Exceptional Houses of Furlow
Gatewood*, by Julia Reed

Cecil Beaton at Home: An Interior Life, by Andrew Ginger

An Affair with a House, by Bunny Williams

British Designers at Home, by Jenny Rose-Innes

Creating a Home, by Kathryn M Ireland

*Designing History: The Extraordinary Art & Style of the
Obama White House*, by Michael S Smith

TRAILBLAZING DESIGNERS
& TIMELESS DECORATION FROM
THE PAST

Elsie de Wolfe: A Decorative Life,
by Nina Campbell and Caroline Seebohm

Syrie Maugham: Staging the Glamorous Interior,
by Pauline C Metcalf

*How They Decorated: Inspiration from Great Women of
the Twentieth Century*, by P Gaye Tapp

Parish Hadley: Sixty Years of American Design,
by Sister Parish, Albert Hadley and Christopher Petkanas

Billy Baldwin: The Great American Decorator,
by Adam Lewis

Nancy Lancaster: English Country House Style,
by Martin Wood

PATTERN & TEXTILES

Near and Far: Interiors I Love, by Lisa Fine

Kit Kemp: Design Thread, by Kit Kemp

David Hicks on Decoration – with Fabrics,
by David Hicks

FOLLOWING – *Sybil, Francesca and Daphne playing in the garden above
the swimming pool at Marnanie.*

Art Credits

6 Robert Doble, *Zephyr*, 2007; artwork on pink wall by Kathleen Ngale; **25, 27, 51, 140–1, 213** Robert Doble, *Tree Studies* series, 2004; **34** Robert Doble, *Daphne*, 2017; **36** Artwork by Celia Perceval; **50** Sidney Nolan, *Upside down bird and insect*, 1984; **53** Robert Healy, prints from the Conolly family series, 18th century; **54** 18th-century lithograph of Coote Castle, Ireland, (artist unknown); **72, 210** Robert Healy, *Grey stallion held by a trainer*, 1768 (print from the Conolly family series); **78** John Mather, *Picnic, Port Phillip Bay Foreshore*, 1903; **95** Robert Doble, *Untitled*, 2011 (private commission); **96** Robert Doble, *Daphne*, 2017 (detail); **110** Artwork by Alfred Saunders; **114** James R Jackson, *Coastal Landscape*, (n.d.); **121** Lantern print from The Winsome Collection, *The Promise of Life*, (original slide c. 1890); **124** Vintage Venetian cat postcards (framed); **128** Artwork by Kathleen Ngale; **138** Robert Doble, *Untitled*, 2011; John Olsen, *Frog and Fly*, 2011; **139** (bottom right) Artwork by Jan Hendrik Scheltema; **161** Clifton Pugh, *Rockpools*, c. 1954; **166–7** Tracy Naughton, *Rochelle* and *Lola* watercolour prints; **173** Robert Doble, *Naphish*, 1998; **177** Artwork above fireplace by Julie Pedler is a reproduction of a painting by C Asquith Baker, which was lost in the fire that destroyed this house; **178–9** Leonard Long, *View Over the River*, 1962; **180–1** Lantern prints from The Winsome Collection, *Racing Yacht Valkyrie England* and *Racing Yacht Satanita England* (original slides c. 1895); **188** Artwork by WL Slack; **191** J Garland, *Snow Mt Macedon*, 1970; **192** John Sanderson-Wells, *Paris*, (n.d.); **203** Sir Edward Lovett Pearce, sketch of console; **204** Antique prints by Henry Alken; **206** John Olsen, *Jacanas – The Christ Bird*, 1983; John Olsen, *Spoonbill and Egret*, 1983; **208–9** Framed prints from the *John Derian Picture Book*; **215** Vintage Indian prints.

Acknowledgements

TO THE CLIENTS I was so lucky to collaborate with on this project:
thank you for your trust in my vision – without you, this book would not exist.

TO GEORDIE TAYLOR: thank you for your support of my career and
allowing me the freedom to create. You are an incredible father and husband,
and I love you very much.

TO MY MOTHER, Andrea Coote: thank you for always believing in me,
listening to me, and for giving me courage to go on.

TO MY STEPFATHER, Alan Naylor: thank you for being the consistent backbone
in my journey. Your wisdom, advice and love has changed my life.

TO JOHN COOTE, wherever you are: thank you for dreaming big
and showing me the way.

TO MY SIBLINGS, Amelia and Angus: thank you for being my counsel
and for all of the laughter.

TO JESSICA PEISLEY: thank you for your incredible ongoing support
and for helping me to bring this book to life.

TO JOHN GRAHAM: thank you for Marnanie and for holding my hand during the
restoration. You are family to Geordie, the girls and me, and we love you very much.

TO PAUL BANGAY: thank you for your endless advice and generosity.
Geordie and I value your friendship enormously.

TO NINA CAMPBELL: thank you for your generous words.
The design world is lucky to have your incredible influence.

TO KIRSTEN ABBOTT AND THE THAMES & HUDSON TEAM: thank you for seeing
my vision for this book and granting me the opportunity to achieve it.

TO CORRIE PERKIN: thank you for your belief in this book and in me.
I am so grateful.

TO RENÉ KRAMERS: thank you for generously gifting your images. You will always
be part of our family.

TO LISA COHEN AND TESS NEWMAN-MORRIS: thank you for being so fun to
create photographs with, and for your cleverness and creative genius.

TO MICHAEL BYRNE AND ALL THE GARDENERS AT MARNANIE:
thank you.

First published in Australia in 2022
by Thames & Hudson Australia Pty Ltd
11 Central Boulevard, Portside Business Park
Port Melbourne, Victoria 3207
ABN: 72 004 751 964

First published in the United Kingdom in 2022
by Thames & Hudson Ltd
181a High Holborn
London WC1V 7QX

First published in the United States of America in 2022
by Thames & Hudson Inc.
500 Fifth Avenue
New York, New York 10110

Thames & Hudson Australia wishes to acknowledge that
Aboriginal and Torres Strait Islander people are the first
storytellers of this nation and the traditional custodians of
the land on which we live and work. We acknowledge their
continuing culture and pay respect to Elders past, present
and future.

ISBN 978-1-760-76156-1

ISBN 978-1-760-76254-4 (U.S. edition)

A catalogue record for this
book is available from the
National Library of Australia

British Library Cataloguing-in-Publication Data
A catalogue record for this book is available from the
British Library

Library of Congress Control Number 2021945413

Every effort has been made to trace accurate ownership
of copyrighted text and visual materials used in this book.
Errors or omissions will be corrected in subsequent editions,
provided notification is sent to the publisher.

Front cover: The pink dining room at Marnanie. Photo by
Lisa Cohen Photography.
Endpapers: Schumacher Sinhala Linen Print
in Pomegranate

Design: Ashlea O'Neill | Salt Camp Studio
Editing: Jessica Redman
Printed and bound in China by C&C Offset Printing Co., Ltd.

FSC® is dedicated to the promotion of responsible forest
management worldwide. This book is made of material
from FSC®-certified forests and other controlled sources.

Be the first to know about our new releases,
exclusive content and author events by visiting

thamesandhudson.com.au
thamesandhudson.com
thamesandhudsonusa.com

Photography credits

Earl Carter: p. 20

Lisa Cohen: pp. 2, 10–13, 21, 31–2, 36–40, 42–95, 98–118,
120–65, 168–74, 176–88, 191–2, 194–9, 201–2, 204–15, 218–21

René Kramers: pp. 22–9, 200, 203

Abbie Melle: pp. 6, 9, 14, 16–17

Hannah Puechmarin: pp. 119, 166–7

Simon Strong: pp. 34, 96

Charlotte Coote's online interior design course
can be found at **themountainacademy.com.au**